Emile Zola

by Philip D. Walker

Professor of French
University of California
Santa Barbara

LONDON

ROUTLEDGE & KEGAN PAUL

NEW YORK: HUMANITIES PRESS

First published 1968
by Routledge and Kegan Paul Ltd
Broadway House, 68–74 Carter Lane
London, E.C.4

Printed in Great Britain
by Northumberland Press Limited
Gateshead

SBN 7100 6225 7 (C)
SBN 7100 6228 1 (P)

The Profiles in Literature Series

This series is designed to provide the student of literature and the general reader with a brief and helpful introduction to the major novelists and prose writers in English, American and foreign literature.

Each volume will provide an account of an individual author's writing career and works, through a series of carefully chosen extracts illustrating the major aspects of the author's art. These extracts are accompanied by commentary and analysis, drawing attention to particular features of the style and treatment. There is no pretence, of course, that a study of extracts can give a sense of the works as a whole, but this selective approach enables the reader to focus his attention upon specific features, and to be informed in his approach by experienced critics and scholars who are contributing to the series.

The volumes will provide a particularly helpful and practical form of introduction to writers whose works are extensive or which present special problems for the modern reader, who can then proceed with a sense of his bearings and an informed eye for the writer's art.

An important feature of these books is the extensive reference list of the author's works and the descriptive list of the most useful biographies, commentaries and critical studies.

B.C.S.

Acknowledgments

The author and publisher wish to thank the following for permission to reprint extracts from copyright works:

Elek Books Ltd.: *Savage Paris* (*Le Ventre de Paris*) trans. David Hughes and Marie-Jacqueline Mason; *A Love Affair* (*Une Page d'Amour*) trans. Jean Stewart; *Earth* (*La Terre*) trans. Ann Lindsay; *The Beast in Man* (*La Bête Humaine*) trans. Alec Brown; *Doctor Pascal* (*Le Docteur Pascal*) trans. Brian Rhys.

Penguin Books Ltd.: *Thérèse Raquin* and *Germinal*, both translated by L. W. Tancock.

Acknowledgment should also be made to Chatto and Windus, publishers of the Vizetelly translations of Zola, of which the following have been used in this volume: *La Faute de l'Abbé Mouret* (*Abbé Mouret's Transgression*); *L'Assommoir* (*The Dram-Shop*); *La Débâcle* (*The Downfall*); Verité (*Truth*); Fécondité (*Fruitfulness*).

Contents

CONTENTS

CONTENTS

                                                      ix

CONTENTS

Emile Zola—his life and works

Zola has recently been rediscovered, especially by the younger generation.

The reasons for this revival, which has astonished many older readers, are not all, of course, exclusively aesthetic. Any writer who paints as angrily and vividly as Zola the darker aspects of modern civilisation must inevitably today arouse widespread interest.

But, at the same time, many of us have also come to realise that Zola is a far better artist (even in the narrower sense) than was once commonly supposed. Far from being mere vulgarised history, social tracts, or crude slices of life, his best works are vast 'poems', closer in spirit to Rimbaud and Baudelaire than to Maupassant and Daudet. They are as stylised and structured as a painting by Zola's boyhood friend Cézanne. In them, poetic, realistic, popular and Parnassian elements are fused together into an extraordinarily powerful synthesis. Zola is a master of the art of reconciling apparently incompatible things. More skilfully than any other writer he meets one of the peculiar needs of our age, which is for a form of fiction which will appeal to our modern desire to be scientific while satisfying the eternal human hunger for legend, fantasy, and myth.

Who exactly was Zola? What are his major works? And what are they about?

The formative years

He was born in Paris on April 2, 1840. His father, Francesco Zola, was an adventurous Italian engineer who had left his native Venice as a young man, lived in Austria, spent time in the French Foreign Legion, and finally settled in France. His mother, Emilie-Aurélie Aubert, was a glazier's daughter from Dourdan.

When he was still very small his family moved to Aix-en-Provence, where his father had conceived the ambitious project of building a canal to supply the city with water. Although the canal has since been completed, his father fell ill and died shortly after work was started, leaving his mother little more than a few worthless stocks. As the years passed, her poverty grew increasingly more severe until at last she had nothing left at all and was forced to throw herself upon the mercy of his father's old associates and friends.

It must not be supposed, however, that the novelist's childhood at Aix was entirely unhappy. In later years he was to remember with nostalgia his friendships with Cézanne and other boys; and he would often recall the many hours they had spent together swimming, tramping around the picturesque Provençal countryside, or reading romantic poetry under its blue skies. He has left us more than one idyllic description of its wild gardens, dusty roads, hot sun, pools, and shady woods which, imbued as he was with the pagan tradition, he peopled with imaginary nymphs and satyrs and liked to compare with ancient Italy and Greece. All in all, the poet in Zola is as deeply rooted in the south of France as in the Paris of the Second Empire. If the capital of Louis Napoleon tended to turn him into a modern Juvenal or Lucretius, Aix is partly responsible for certain enduring traits in his verse, fiction, and opera librettos reminiscent perhaps of Longus or Ovid.

His mother, in her desperate search for a way out of her financial difficulties, returned to Paris in December, 1857. In February, 1858, after selling what remained of the furniture, he rejoined her and was soon enrolled as a scholarship pupil at the Lycée Saint-Louis. Although he had so far done well at school, winning prizes in Greek, Latin, and other subjects, he now failed to pass the oral examinations required for the baccalaureate degree. One of the reasons was undoubtedly his poor health. In November, 1858 he had come down with a serious malady that had dragged on for about two months. The *Journal of a Convalescent* which he wrote afterwards contains vivid descriptions of nightmares and hallucinations undoubtedly based on his own experiences during this illness. They suggest to what a great extent he was already obsessed at the age of eighteen, by some of the most persistent poetic themes and images underlying his novels: the struggle of life against death, the theme of death and resurrection, and the double image of burial alive and the bursting of seeds through soil.

After his failure at school—it was a professor of literature who refused to pass him!—he worked for a while at a dull, poorly paid clerk's job on the Paris Docks. But he quit in disgust and for well over a year lived the life of a Bohemian. In some ways it was the grimmest period of his existence. Often, during the abnormally harsh winters of 1860–61 and 1861–62 he had to keep to his bed to stay warm. On at least one occasion he was obliged to pawn his clothes; and many a time he had nothing to eat but a little bread dipped in oil. He also had an unhappy affair with a young prostitute whom he had hoped to save through the power of love—a hopelessly idealistic adventure that did much to further his education as a realist. Yet, despite these grim circumstances, he managed during these first years in Paris to read and absorb Dante, Montaigne, Hugo, Shakespeare, Rabelais, Lamartine, Chénier, Michelet, and many other authors and to write a considerable number of stories and poems.

Wrestling, as he would all his life, with the problem of how to achieve immortality, he contemplated writing a book to be entitled *The Poet*, in which he would try to isolate and analyse exactly what it was the great poets of humanity all had in common. His ambition was to emulate, but not imitate, Homer. In September, 1860 he wrote to Augustin Baille at Aix:

The epic poem—I mean my own sort of epic poem and not a stupid imitation of the Ancients—would seem to be a sufficiently original possibility. It is plain enough to me that each society has its own particular kind of poetry; now, since our society is different from that of 1830 and does not yet have its own poetry, the man who finds it will be famous. Our hopes in a better tomorrow, the winds of liberty stirring all around us, religion in the process of purifying itself—these are all, without any doubt, powerful sources of inspiration. The whole trick is to find a new form, to sing about the man of the future in the proper way, to portray with grandeur humanity mounting the steps of the sanctuary. You must agree that there is something sublime to be found in all that. But what it is I don't quite know yet. I feel the presence of some imposing figure stirring in the darkness, but I cannot yet make out its precise features. . . .

He doggedly hammered out hundreds of verses. He dreamed up impossible projects: among others, a trilogy, *Genesis*, in three cantos, the first to be entitled *The Birth of the World*, the second, *Humanity*, and the third, *The Man of the Future*. He managed with infinite pain to compose only the merest beginning. Yet this brief fragment tells us a great deal about his innermost motives. It should be printed at the head of every complete edition of his mature creative work. For what are the *Rougon-Macquart* novels, the *Three Cities*, and the *Four Gospels* if not the realisation, in different forms, of his youthful epic ambitions?

The Birth of the World

Creative Principle, unique First Force,
Who with the breath of life made matter animate,
Thou who live, knowing neither birth nor death,
Give me the golden wing of the inspired prophet.
I shall sing of thy work and on it traced
In time and space I shall read thy thought.
I shall rise towards thee, born upwards on thy breath
To offer thee this mortal song of immortality.

In late 1861, a family friend took pity on him and helped him get a job at Hachette's publishing house, where he was promptly promoted to a clerkship in the publicity department. During his Bohemian years, he had been chiefly absorbed in discovering his own poetic ambitions. His main energies now went into attuning his poetic genius with his age. He read, among other important writers of the age, Taine, Renan, Darwin, Stendhal, Balzac, and

Flaubert. Through Cézanne, he was introduced into artistic circles and would be a familiar figure at the Café Guerbois, the cradle of modern painting. His position as publicity chief at Hachette's taught him what goes on in the back rooms of the publishing world, helped him meet many leading authors, and put him into contact with editors.

Early writings

In October, 1864 his first book came out, *Stories for Ninon*, a collection of largely romantic short pieces. In 1865 he published his first novel, *Claude's Confession*, a fictionalised account of his disillusioning affair with the girl he had taken in off the streets.

In 1866, he resigned from Hachette's and for several years supported himself through journalism. He became the principal champion of Manet and the Impressionists, and in the process turned himself into a leading art critic. He reviewed an endless stream of books, often reading three or four a day. He was an original drama critic. He commented on the life of the capital, transmitted gossip, took part in public debates.

Altogether, his journalistic writings fill several volumes and present a fascinating picture of the political and cultural life of a whole epoch. Through them we may glimpse, often as vividly as in his novels, the corrupt, showy, materialistic, infinitely vulgar society of the time —the pompous, parvenu court of the man whom Victor Hugo in glorious exile called 'Napoleon the Small' and the whole swarming throng of Second Empire social climbers, politicians, big promoters, courtesans, Academicians, aesthetes, and roués. We see the luxurious carriages, the masked balls and midnight orgies, the concert halls resounding with the brassy music of Offenbach (which

Zola detested). We take part in the quarrels between Academic painters and Impressionists. We meet the major poets, critics, novelists, and intellectuals. We also see Zola sharpening his own faculties, perfecting his style, developing his theories.

Convinced as he was that the only way to become a truly great artist was to be blessed, first of all, with a powerful and original temperament and, secondly, to find the form best suited to one's own times, he was increasingly certain that the right form for his own century was not verse, but the novel, which he regarded as the modern descendant of the Greek epic. In a scientific age, moreover, he felt that the artist must exploit the artistic possibilities of science. His description of Flaubert in *La Tribune* (28 November 1869) as 'a Titan, with giant lungs bursting with breath, who recounts the mores of an ant-hill, while making enormous efforts not to succumb to a desire to play heroic music on his great bronze trumpet. . . . A poet changed into a naturalist, Homer become Cuvier' undoubtedly tells us less about Flaubert than it does about Zola's own evolving ideal of what a modern novelist should be.

Meanwhile he continued writing fiction (as well as an occasional play) and in 1870 brought out in serialised form the first of the series of twenty novels which was to be his major achievement: *Les Rougon-Macquart, the Natural and Social History of a Family During the Second Empire*. It is clear from his more public pronouncements that he wanted to create the impression that these were primarily social and physiological studies based on observation and the laws of inheritance. He carefully fostered the myth that the plots of his novels grew logically out of his scientific observations, which, he implied, came first in the development of each work. In actual practice, however, he was quite capable of drawing up at least a partial outline of a plot before seriously beginning to gather his realistic data. Indeed, the more deeply we go into the genesis of most of his novels, the more it becomes apparent that they are essentially developments of some poetic idea.

The first volume in the series, *The Rougons' Luck*, is a dramatic description of the *coup d'état* of 1851 as it affected a provincial town. It is told through the dramatic frame of a love story reminiscent (as Zola himself was quite aware) of certain famous Greek romances.

The second novel, *The Kill* (made into a film by Roger Vadim, *The Game is Over*) portrays the shady world of high finance through a dramatic plot based on the ancient mythological theme of Phaedra.

Volume III, *Savage Paris* (1873) a vast still life about the central food markets of Paris, transforms them into the 'belly' of a personified Paris and, by extension, the symbol of the Second Empire bourgeoisie calmly digesting its wealth and, finally, the Second Empire itself.

The fifth book, *The Sinful Priest* (1875) is about a young priest who, after an attack of amnesia, falls in love with a wild, half-mythical girl in a vast ruined garden named Paradou—an elaborate adaptation of the story of Adam and Eve.

In short, work after work turns out to be the development in realistic terms of an essentially poetic idea.

It is not surprising that, despite his naturalistic theories and convictions, many of Zola's friends and admirers were poets. In his late twenties he made the acquaintance of Verlaine, whose poetic genius he recognised and praised. When his first publisher, Lacroix, went bankrupt shortly after the publication of *The Kill* in 1872, it was the ageing Gautier who helped persuade Charpentier to take over where Lacroix had left off. In 1874, Mallarmé, always one of Zola's most devoted readers, asked him to contribute to *La Dernière Mode*, a review which he had just founded. Somewhat later, Mallarmé showed once again his respect for Zola by bringing *His Excellency, Eugène Rougon* (1876), a novel about the political world, to the attention of his friend O'Shaughnessy, in the hope that he would review it in the London *Athenaeum*.

Zola's naturalism

Nevertheless, Zola's naturalistic propaganda gradually created a popular image of him as an anti-poetic realist, a scientist who had little serious use for the poetic imagination. Following the world-wide success of *L'Assommoir* (1877), the grim story of a laundress married to a drunkard and finally reduced to prostitution in the slums of Paris, he fired off a number of articles (*The Experimental Novel*, 1880) which were essentially manifestos and, like most manifestos, made some excessive statements—statements which he himself would not take very seriously in later years. He even went so far as to picture the ideal novelist as not only a scientific *observer*, but also an *experimenter*, contributing to human knowledge by conducting scientific experiments on fictional people. But some of the ideas Zola expresses in *The Experimental Novel* are not quite so ridiculous as many critics have made them out to be. We must, however, always distinguish very carefully between Zola's naturalist theories and his actual practice. A much more revealing definition of what he really does in his novels than all the essays in *The Experimental Novel* put together is a letter which he wrote on March 22, 1885 to Henry Céard:

You are not surprised, like the others, to discover a

poet in me. . . . We all lie more or less, but what are
the mechanics and the mentality of our Lie? Now—and
I may be wrong—but I believe that as far as my own
lie is concerned it leads to a fuller understanding of the
truth. I have an obsession with true details, the leap
into the stars from the springboard of exact observation.
Truth mounts on a single stroke of the wing all the way
up to the realm of symbol.

Nana (1880) is much more than a simple realistic por-
trait of a Second Empire prostitute who becomes the toast
of Paris and then, after destroying her rich lovers, dies
of smallpox; it is a symbolic portrayal of the revenge of
the slums on the corrupt society which has created them.

Germinal (1885)—one of the world's greatest masterpieces—is not just a story about a strike in the coal mines.
It is a prose epic conveying through a portrayal of a typical
mine community an objective analysis of the labour problem and a subjective vision of history, man, and nature.

Earth (1887), an intensely pure book, despite its crude
words and so-called obscenity, is, again, essentially a profound poetic vision. 'I want,' Zola wrote in his notes, 'to
write the living poem of the earth, but without symbolism,
humanly. I mean by that that I want to show, first of all,
the peasant's love for the earth, an immediate love, the
desire to possess as much of the earth as possible, to have
a lot of it, because for him it represents wealth. Then, on
a somewhat higher level, I want to portray the peasant's
love for the all-nourishing earth, the earth from which
we take all that we have—our being, our substance, our
life—and to which we finally return.'

The Beast in Man (1890), another of Zola's best works,
is a nightmarish novel about the railroads, the judicial
system, and dark, elemental human passions. One of the

main characters is Nana's brother Jacques Lantier, a psychopathic locomotive driver, who has to kill the woman he loves. The novel is constructed uniquely on two *Rougon-Macquart* myths—the myth of blood and the myth of catastrophe. The railroad and its locomotives are animated and transformed by Zola into powerful poetic symbols.

The Downfall (1892), a novel about the Franco-Prussian War, the Paris Commune, and the tragic friendship of two soldiers, transforms the war and the disasters which followed it into symbols of national death and resurrection.

After completing the *Rougon-Macquart* series, Zola wrote a trilogy full of symbolism and prophetic visions, *The Three Cities: Lourdes* (1894), *Rome* (1896), and *Paris* (1898). They are tied together by a loose plot about a priest who has lost his faith and tries unsuccessfully to regain it.

In 1898 his heroic defence of Captain Dreyfus made him one of the most loved and hated men in French history. After his return from England, where he had to flee as a result of his intervention, he began still another series of novels, *The Four Gospels*, but finished only three: *Fruitfulness* (1899), *Work* (1901), and *Truth* (1903). They portray his dream of a better world made possible by a respect for the natural forces of fecundity (he is against birth control), human labour, and science and education.

He died in 1902. At his funeral, Anatole France called him 'a moment of the conscience of man', and huge crowds shouting *'Germinal!' 'Germinal!'* passed by his grave. In 1908 his ashes were transferred to the Pantheon.

He is one of the best proofs that we have that the ancient spirit of poetry, in the deepest and widest sense, not only survives in our modern scientific, technological world, but is still capable of taking its rightful place at the very centre of society.

Scheme of extracts

People don't read me, that's for sure—at least they don't read me intelligently; and I suspect that twenty or fifty years after my death I shall be discovered.

(Zola, 1895)

There are many ways of reading a novel. But if our purpose is to go straight to the heart of an author we must select the approach most likely to succeed in his particular case. Fortunately, Zola himself has left us some important clues insofar as his own writing is concerned. One is his famous definition of art as a corner of nature seen through a temperament; i.e., a certain kind of distortion, or 'lie'. Another is his confession to Henry Céard (see p. 9 above) that his own fiction is a very special sort of lie which presents in the guise of one kind of truth ('realism') an even greater kind of truth ('poetry').

If this is indeed the case—and most students of Zola will agree on this—it is obvious that to read Zola as he should be read, we must start out by distinguishing as well as we can (and this is not always easy or even perhaps possible) between the realistic elements in his fiction

12

and the more clearly poetic ones. We must grasp the essential characteristics of each, attempting among other things to discover what kinds of truth are involved. And, finally, we must explore the different ways poetry and realism are combined in his work.

This is what this book is designed to help the reader do.

Part I contains a collection of abstracts illustrative of Zola's poetic side, beginning with a section in which the main emphasis is somewhat more on his more *formal* or *technical* poetic characteristics than on the specific poetic content of his novels: e.g., his love of strong rhythmic effects; his use of different kinds of traditional poetic imagery; his use of the romantic and symbolist device of synesthesia; his tendency to create new 'myths' or to adapt specific ancient myths; his penchant for transforming his characters into symbols; his lyrical and epical traits. There then follow examples illuminating primarily the poetic *content* of his fiction or his poetic vision of man and nature; e.g., his unanimism or the sense of world destruction and renewal that pervades his work.

Part II contains a number of extracts illustrative of his realism. In this part, I have begun with examples of the different kinds of realistic verisimilitude that he achieves —e.g., historical authenticity, conformation with scientific theory or representation of phenomena as they occur in the consciousness of persons in abnormal psychological states. In the following pages I have provided extracts intended primarily to illustrate some of the most important realistic themes and subjects that he treats. I then conclude with a very tentative indication (in which my debt to the late Erich Auerbach is obvious) of what may well be Zola's most significant achievement in the light of the European realistic tradition taken as a whole.

In Part III, I have indicated, again with examples, one

or two of the most characteristic ways in which the poetic and realistic ingredients of Zola's fiction are combined. Since discovering for oneself how he does this—what might be termed seeing through Zola's lie—is one of the chief pleasures that may be derived from reading him, I have deliberately made this section very short, limiting myself to his less well-kept secrets.

As for the reasons why I have chosen to include certain extracts and not others, I can only say that I have been guided first and foremost by the desire to choose the best examples that I could find, according to my own taste. Some of them, like the crowd scenes from *Germinal* or the description of a working-class dwelling in *L'Assommoir*, are already quite famous. Others, less often cited, deserve —I think the reader will concur—to be better known.

Part One: The Poet

Sense of rhythm

Although Zola writes in prose, he has a poet's love for measure, repetition, and proportion and is a master of the art of creating strongly rythmic effects. *Earth*, for example, begins with this powerful description of the slow, rhythmic motion of a sower accompanied by the equally rhythmic cracks of a waggoner's whip.

I

That morning, Jean was in the fields, holding open with his left hand a blue canvas seedbag knotted round his waist; with his right he brought out a fistful of corn and scattered it broadcast with a single flick of the wrist, every three steps. As he swung rhythmically along, his heavy clogs sank in the rich soil and came away thickly-caked. And at each throw, through the ceaselessly flying golden grain, gleamed the two red stripes on the sleeve of the army jacket he was wearing out. He strode on in solitary grandeur; and a harrow slowly followed, burying the seeds. Two horses, whom the waggoner urged on with long regular whipcracks over the ears, were harnessed to the harrow.

Earth (1887), Part I, ch. i

Similarly, another of his greatest novels, *Germinal*, starts out with a highly rhythmic chapter in which he evokes at fairly regular intervals the recurrent gusts of the March wind sweeping across a vast frozen plain, the panting sound made by the exhaust-pipe of a coal mine, and the violent coughing fits of an old man. In each of these two works he employs rhythm much as a composer does in the overture of a musical composition—to set the over-all pace and mood of what is to follow.

Use of imagery

Zola habitually resorts to figurative language to portray reality, express a poetic vision, or convey a mood. This passage, in which Paris is described as it might appear at dawn through the eyes of a woman falling in love, is a good example.

2

That morning, Paris was awakening lazily, with a smile. A mist lay along the Seine valley, submerging both banks. It was a light milky vapour, which grew brighter as the sun gained strength. Nothing of the town could be made out under this airy floating muslin veil. In the hollows where the cloud lay thicker, it assumed a darker, bluish tinge, while over wide spaces it thinned out to a delicate transparent film, a haze of golden dust through which the channel of the streets could be guessed at; and above it rose the grey shapes of domes and spires, breaking through the mist, still wrapped in shreds of the vapour they had pierced. Now and then great puffs of yellow smoke would drift upwards like gigantic slow-moving birds and then melt into the air, which seemed to absorb them. And above this immense expanse, above the cloud that hung and slumbered over Paris, spread the lofty, pure vault of the sky, so palely blue that it was almost white. The sun climbed up, its radiance a soft shimmer. A pale light, like the cloudy gold of a child's hair, streamed like rain, filling the wide air with its tremulous warmth. Infinite space seemed to rejoice, supremely peaceful and tenderly gay, while the town, riddled by countless golden arrows, lay idly drowsing, reluctant to cast aside the lace that covered it.

Hélène, for the past week, had enjoyed the sight of the great city thus spread out before her. She never tired of it. It was unsoundable and various as an ocean, innocently bright in the morning and aflame at night, assuming the joyous or melancholy mood of the skies it reflected. A burst of sunshine would set it rippling with floods of gold, a cloud would darken it, awakening stormy turbulence. It was constantly new; in a dead calm it would glow orange, under a sudden squall turn leaden grey from end to end, bright clear weather would set the crest of every house-top sparkling, while rainstorms drowned heaven and earth and wiped out the horizon in chaotic disaster. For Hélène it held all the melancholy and all the hope of the open sea; she even fancied she felt the sharp breath and the tang of the sea against her face; and the very sound of the city, its low continuous roar, brought her the illusion of the rising tide beating against the rocks of a cliff.

The book slid from her hands while she sat day-dreaming, her gaze far away. When she let it fall thus, it was because she felt a need to pause in her reading, to think things over, to wait. She took delight in keeping her curiosity unsatisfied for a while. The story filled her with overwhelming emotion. And Paris, that morning, reflected the joy and the vague uneasiness of her own heart. She found it very sweet to remain in ignorance, half-guessing, yielding to a slow initiation, with an ill-defined sense that her youth was beginning again.

18

What lies these novels told! Of course she was right never to read them. They were fairy-stories fit for empty-headed people with no sense of reality. And yet she could not resist the book's attraction; her thoughts dwelt inevitably on the passionate love of those two women, Rebecca the lovely Jewess and noble Lady Rowena, for the knight Ivanhoe. It seemed to her that she would have loved as proudly as Rowena, with the same patient serenity. Love, love! and the unspoken word, which instinctively thrilled through her whole being, surprised her and made her smile. In the distance pale fleecy clouds drifted over Paris, borne on a breeze, like a flock of swans. Great sheets of mist were moving away; for one instant the left bank appeared, hazy and shimmering like a fairy city seen in a dream; but a mass of vapour sank down and the city was swallowed up as though in a flood. Now the mist spread evenly over all districts, forming a fine lake with smooth white water. Only a denser current marked the course of the Seine with a grey sinuous line. Over these white, calm waters, shadows floated slowly, like ships with rosy sails; and the young woman's eyes followed their course, dreamily. Love, love! and she watched her floating dream, with a smile.

A Love Affair (1878), Part I, ch. v

What may particularly strike the student of Zola's style in this description is the skilful use he makes of simile and metaphor to evoke fleeting effects of light and shadow, creating a literary equivalent of an Impressionist painting. But one may also note the almost hallucinatory quality he achieves through the personification of Paris in the first paragraph and, in the second paragraph, the hyperbolic comparison between the city and the sea. Finally, one may remark the way he exploits details from the physical setting to reflect Hélène's subjective state as she looks up dreamily from her copy of *Ivanhoe*. It is obvious that in this novel, which Mallarmé regarded as an 'uninterrupted poem', Paris is made to perform a very special function, not very different, as Zola himself points out in a preface, from that of a classical Chorus: 'From my twentieth year I dreamed of writing a novel in which Paris, with its sea of roofs, would be one of the characters, something like the Chorus in classical antiquity. I needed an intimate drama, three or four creatures in a small room and then the immense town on the horizon, always present, watching these creatures laugh and weep, with its eyes of stone. . . .'

Fancy

Zola shared with the public of his day a taste for fantasy and injected elements of a fanciful nature into even his most realistic novels. In the following scene from *The Downfall*, for example, French cuirassiers crossing the Meuse during the Franco-Prussian war are transformed in his imagination into awesome figures straight out of folklore and legend.

3

The fires on both banks had blazed up more brightly, and their glare was so intense that the whole fearful scene could now be made out in nightmarish detail. The pontoons had settled to such an extent, under the weight of the cavalry and artillery which had been crossing uninterruptedly since morning, that the superstructure of the bridge was covered with water a few inches deep. The cuirassiers were passing at the moment, two abreast, in a long unbroken file, emerging from the darkness as they reached the river and disappearing into the darkness on the other side, and nothing could be seen of the bridge; they seemed to be marching on the water, this violently lighted water with its dancing flames. The horses neighed, their manes bristling with terror, their legs stiffening as they felt that strange terrain shift and yield under their hoofs. The cuirassiers, standing erect in their stirrups and keeping a tight rein, kept on crossing, ceaselessly crossing, wrapped in their great white mantles, their helmets alone visible, flashing in the red light of the flames. You might have taken them for some spectral band of knights, with locks of fire, going forth to do battle with the powers of darkness.

The Downfall (1892), Part I, ch. vii

Synesthesia

Like Baudelaire and other nineteenth-century poets Zola occasionally applies words associated with one kind of sensation to sensations of a different nature. When, for instance, he recounts the death of Albine in *Abbé Mouret's Transgression*, he uses terms normally applied to music to describe the fragrance of the flowers with which she deliberately suffocates herself.

4

For a moment she remained standing, glancing around her. She was looking to see if death was there. And she gathered up the aromatic greenery, the southernwood, the mint, the verbenas, the balm, and the fennel. She broke them and twisted them and made wedges of them with which to stop up every little chink and cranny about the windows and the door. Then she drew the white coarsely sewn calico curtains and, without even a sigh, laid herself upon the bed, on all the florescence of hyacinths and tuberoses.

And then a final rapture was granted her. With her eyes wide open she smiled at the room. Ah! how she had loved there! And how happily she was there going to die! At that supreme moment the plaster cupids suggested nothing impure to her; the amorous paintings disturbed her no more. She was conscious of nothing beneath that blue ceiling save the intoxicating perfume of the flowers. And it seemed to her as if this perfume was none other than the old love-fragrance which had always warmed the room, now increased a hundredfold, till it had become so strong and penetrating that it would surely suffocate her. Perchance it was the breath of the lady who had died there a century ago. In perfect stillness, with her hands clasped over her heart, she continued smiling, while she listened to the whispers of the perfumes in her buzzing head. They were singing to her a soft strange melody of fragrance, which slowly and very gently lulled her to sleep.

At first there was a prelude, bright and childlike; her hands, that had just now twisted and twined the aromatic greenery, exhaled the pungency of crushed herbage, and recalled her old girlish ramblings through the wildness of the Paradou. Then there came a flutelike song, a song of short musky notes, rising from the violets that lay upon the table near the head of the bed; and this flutelike strain, trilling melodiously to the soft accompaniment of the lilies on the other table, sang to her of the first joys of love, its first confession, and first kisses beneath the trees of the forest. But she began to stifle as passion drew nigh with the clovelike breath of the carnations, which burst upon her in brazen notes that seemed to drown all others. She thought that death was nigh when the poppies and the marigolds broke into a wailing strain, which recalled the torment of desire. But suddenly all grew quieter; she felt that she could breathe more freely; she glided into greater serenity, lulled by a descending scale that came from the throats of the stocks, and died away amidst a delightful hymn from the heliotropes, which, with their vanilla-like breath, proclaimed the approach of nuptial bliss. Here and there the mirabilis gently trilled. Then came a hush. And afterwards the roses languidly made their entry. Their voices streamed from the ceiling, like the strains of a distant choir. It was a chorus of great breadth, to which she at first listened with a slight quiver. Then the volume of the strain increased, and soon her whole frame vibrated with the mighty sounds that burst in waves around her. The nuptials were at hand, the trumpet blasts of the roses announced them. She pressed her hands more closely to her heart as she lay there panting, gasping, dying. When she opened her lips for the kiss which was to stifle her, the hyacinths and tuberoses shot out their perfume and enveloped her with so deep, so great a sigh that the chorus of the roses could be heard no more.

And then, amidst the final gasp of the flowers, Albine died.

Abbé Mouret's Transgression (1875), Part III, ch. xiv

Reading this passage, one may think particularly of Baudelaire's famous poem *Correspondences*:

> . . . perfumes fresh as the flesh of children,
> Sweet as the oboe, green as prairies.

At least one major authority on the symbolist movement has suggested that *Abbé Mouret's Transgression* must be regarded as a primarily symbolist novel despite Zola's reputation as the chief of the French naturalists.

Mythopoeism

Zola not only develops in his novels themes traditionally associated with myth—e.g., world creation, destruction, and renewal, descents into the lower regions of the earth, battles between heroes and monsters—but often does so through images and symbols which themselves assume something of the compelling force of myth. When, for example, in *Germinal* a courageous anarchist sabotages a mine by weakening the wooden pit lining holding back a subterranean water deposit, the pit is metaphorically transformed into the throat of a giant beast.

5

The job demanded an incredible nerve, and a score of times he all but overbalanced and fell the hundred and eighty metres to the bottom. He had had to get a hold on the oaken guides in which the cages slid up and down, and even turned upside down, simply buttressing himself with an elbow or a knee, and with a cool contempt for death. A mere breath would have upset him, and three times he just caught himself in time without so much as a shudder. First he explored with his hands and then did his work, only lighting a match when he had lost his bearings among these greasy timbers. Having loosened the screws he attacked the planking itself, and the danger became even greater. He had found the key piece which held all the others and concentrated on that, boring, sawing, and thinning to lessen its resistance, and all the time water spurted through the holes and slits in fine jets of icy rain which blinded him and soaked him through. Two matches were put out and then the whole box got wet, and there was nothing but impenetrable night.

Then he worked like one possessed. The breath of the invisible elated him, and the black horror of this rain-swept cavern filled him with a frenzy of destruction. He attacked the lining at random, hitting wherever he could, using his brace and bit or his saw as though his one idea were to rip everything open there and then on top of him. He put into the task the sort of ferocity with which he might have driven a knife into the flesh of some living being whom he loathed. He would kill this foul beast in the end, this pit with the ever-open jaws that had swallowed down so much human flesh. The bite of his tools could be heard as he stretched himself out, crawled along, went down, came up, holding on by a miracle, in continual movement like some night bird flying in and out between the beams of a belfry.

But he forced himself to take things calmly. Surely he could keep a cool head? He quietly waited to recover his breath, and then moved back into the escape shaft, filling up the gap by replacing the panel he had sawn out. That would do. He did not want to raise the alarm by doing too much damage at that moment, for they might have tried to repair it at once. Sufficient that the beast was wounded in the vitals, and whether it would still be alive by the next evening remained to be seen. What was more, he had put his signature to the job, so that a horrified world should know that the pit had not died a natural death.

Germinal (1885), Part VII, ch. ii

Adaptation of specific myths

Occasionally Zola may be found exploiting classical and Judeo-Christian mythology in order to express his own radically modern vision. *Abbé Mouret's Transgression*, for example, is a violently anticlerical, anti-Christian version of the story of Adam and Eve. In the idyllic setting of a gone-to-seed eighteenth-century garden named Paradou, Albine, Zola's Eve, leads the young Abbé Serge Mouret, his Adam, to a tree which may recall not so much the tree of the knowledge of good and evil, perhaps, as the equally legendary tree of life, symbol of a fertile and beneficient Nature.

6

Then Albine and Serge instinctively raised their heads. In front of them they beheld a colossal mass of foliage; and, as they hesitated for a moment, a roe, after gazing at them with its sweet soft eyes, bounded into the thickets.

'It is there,' said Albine.

She led the way, her face again turned towards Serge, whom she drew with her, and they disappeared amid the quivering leaves, and all grew quiet again. They were entering into delicious peace.

In the centre there stood a tree covered with so dense a foliage that one could not recognise its species. It was of giant girth, with a trunk that seemed to breathe like a living breast, and far-reaching boughs that stretched like protecting arms around it. It towered up there beautiful, strong, virile, and fruitful. It was the king of the garden, the father of the forest, the pride of the plants, the beloved of the sun, whose earliest and latest beams smiled daily on its crest. From its green vault poured all the joys of creation: fragrance of flowers, music of birds, gleams of golden light, wakeful freshness of dawn, slumbrous warmth of evening twilight. So strong was the sap that it burst through the very bark, bathing the tree with the powers of fruitfulness, making it the symbol of earth's virility. Its presence sufficed to give the clearing an enchanting charm. The other trees built up around it an impenetrable wall, which isolated it as in a sanctuary of silence and twilight. There was but greenery there, not a scrap of sky, not a glimpse of horizon; nothing but a swelling rotunda, draped with green silkiness of leaves, adorned below with mossy velvet. And one entered, as into the liquid crystal of a source, a greenish limpidity, a sheet of silver reposing beneath reflected reeds. Colours, perfumes, sounds, quivers, all were vague, indeterminate, transparent, steeped in a felicity amidst which everything seemed to faint away. Languorous warmth, the glimmer of a summer's night, as it fades on the bare shoulder of some fair girl, a scarce perceptible murmur of love sinking into silence, lingered beneath the motionless branches, unstirred by the slightest zephyr. It was hymeneal solitude, a chamber where Nature lay hidden in the embraces of the sun.

Albine and Serge stood there in an ecstasy of joy. As soon as the tree had received them beneath its shade, they felt eased of all the anxious disquiet which had so long distressed them. The fears which had made them avoid each other, the fierce wrestling of spirit which had

29

torn and wounded them, without consciousness on their part of what they were really contending against, vanished, and left them in perfect peace. Absolute confidence, supreme serenity, now pervaded them, they yielded unhesitatingly to the joy of being together in that lonely nook, so completely hidden from the outside world. They had surrendered themselves to the garden, they awaited in all calmness the behests of that tree of life. It enveloped them in such ecstasy of love that the whole clearing seemed to disappear from before their eyes, and to leave them wrapped in an atmosphere of perfume.

Abbé Mouret's Transgression, Part II, ch. xv

A similar tendency to adapt and modify traditional mythological material may be observed in many other places in Zola's fiction—e.g., *The Kill*, which he envisaged as a modern *Phaedra*, and above all *Germinal*, where one may discover a surprising number of parallels with Judeo-Christian and Greco-Roman myths (Tartarus and Tartaret, for instance, or the symbolic inundation of the mine and the classical or Biblical flood).

Symbolic development of character

Zola's literary characters are often highly original creations. Many of them, like the figures in much modern painting, appear to be little more upon first acquaintance than enormous, distorted, superhuman silhouettes, void of complication, roughly blocked in, in heavy masses. Yet they frequently assume intense life. This is due, in part, to his technical skill as an animator, and, in part, to their symbolic force. A blacksmith becomes a superhuman symbol of the redemptive power of work. A fishwife is transformed into a disquieting embodiment of the sea. Nana, the prostitute, incarnates the revenge of the slums on the rich and decadent society of the Second Empire.

7

Oh, what a splendid sight the blacksmith was to behold at times those hot afternoons—stripped to the waist, with taut, bulging muscles, like one of those huge figures by Michelangelo that seem to be making a supreme effort to hold themselves erect! I found in the contours of his body the modern sculptural lines that our artists are painfully searching for in the lifeless flesh of Greek statues.

He took on in my eyes the larger than life proportions of a hero of labour, the tireless child of our times, ceaselessly hammering out on his anvil the tools of science and fashioning with fire and iron the world of tomorrow. He played with his hammers as if they were toys. When he felt like having a little fun, he would take the 'Maiden' and strike it with all his might. At such times he would make the whole place resound with his thunder in the rosy breath of the furnace. It seemed to me that I could hear the panting of the whole people at work.

The Blacksmith (1868)

8

She appeared to him colossal in size, very heavy and almost disturbing, with her large breasts; he shifted his pointed elbows and his thin shoulders away, possibly for fear of digging them into this flesh. His thin bones passed through a moment of agony in contact with her plump bodice. He bowed his head and shrunk still more deeply into his chair, restless from the strong scent that rose from her. Whenever her shift hung loosely open, he seemed to see a breath of health and living emerge from between the two white breasts and pass over his face, still warm, as if mingling for a moment with a touch of the stench of the Halles on a boiling July evening. It was a lingering perfume, clinging to the smooth silk of the skin, a sweat of fish flowing from her splendid breasts, her regal arms and supple waist, bringing a sharp tang of something else to her woman's smell. She had tried all the aromatic oils, she washed in running water, but as soon as the freshness of her bathing wore off, her blood conveyed even to the tips of her fingers that insipid presence of salmon, the musk violet of the smelt and the pungency of herring and ray. The swing of her skirts released this vapour; she walked through an evaporation of slimy seaweed; with her handsome body of a goddess, her wonderful paleness and

32

purity, she was like a fine and ancient marble statue rolled in the path of the seas and brought back to the coast in the net of a sardine fisherman. Florent suffered from it. He did not desire her, for his senses were repelled by after-noons in the fish market, and he found her irritating, too salty, too bitter to the taste, too large in her beauty and too stale in the strength of her smell.

Savage Paris (1873), ch. iii

9

She let go her chemise and waited there, naked, while Muffat finished reading Fauchery's article. He read it slowly. It was entitled *The Golden Fly*, and it told the story of a girl descended from four or five generations of drunkards, her blood tainted by a long heredity of poverty and alcoholism, which, in her case, had resulted in a nervous disorder affecting her sexual behaviour. She had grown up in the streets of an impoverished section of Paris, and now, tall, beautiful, with a fine body, like some dung-hill plant, she was avenging all the beggars and poor abandoned wretches from whom she had sprung. With her, the putrescence that was allowed to ferment among the lower classes was rising up and spreading to the aristocracy. She was becoming a force of nature, a ferment of disorganisation, without wishing it, corrupting and destroying Paris between her snow-white thighs, turning it sour as some women, every month, turn milk sour. And it was at the end of the article that he found the com-parison with the fly, a sun-coloured fly that had risen from the dung, a fly that sucked in death on the carrion left to rot on the roadside and then, buzzing, dancing, glitter-ing like a precious stone, flies in through the windows of palaces and poisons the men inside merely by alighting on them.

Muffat raised his head and stared fixedly . . . Yes, she really was that Golden Beast, unaware of her own power, able with her odour alone to taint and corrupt the world. He could not look away, obsessed, possessed, until finally, when he closed his eyes in order not to see, the animal appeared in the depths of the darkness, enlarged, terrible, exaggerating its posture. He knew that it would stay there, before his eyes, in his very flesh, forever.

Nana (1880), ch. vii

Lyricism

Despite his scientific pretensions, Zola is one of the most lyrical of all novelists. He conceived of *Earth*, for example, as a great 'poem' about the soil. The main viewpoint character is Jean Macquart (whom readers of this text have already encountered as the sower in an extract taken from the beginning of this novel). In the final pages, which are remarkable for their sustained lyricism, Jean, after visiting the fresh graves of his brutally murdered wife, Françoise, and father-in-law, Fouan, takes one last look at the land which, after the tragic events that have overtaken him, he plans to leave forever.

10

Jean was left alone. Away in the distance only great reddish clouds of smoke were rising from the ruins of La Borderie, whirling about and throwing cloud-shadows across the ploughed fields and the scattered sowers. His eyes travelled slowly back to the ground at his feet, and he stared at the fresh mounds of earth under which Françoise and Old Fouan now rested. His anger of the morning, his revulsion against men and things, was dissipated, and he felt a profound peace. In spite of himself a sense of gentleness and hope flooded into his heart, perhaps because of the warm sunshine.

His master Hourdequin had made a lot of trouble for himself with new inventions and hadn't had much to gain from his machines, his fertilisers and all the other scientific things which were still so inefficiently applied. Then La Cognette had arrived to finish him off; he too was sleeping in this cemetery; and nothing remained of the farm— the wind was carrying even the ashes away. But what did it matter? Buildings might be burned down, you couldn't burn the earth. The earth, the sustainer, would always remain, and she would go on nourishing those who sowed seed in her. She contained space and time; she would always give corn and was content to wait until men knew how to make her yield even more.

It was just the same with the prophecies of revolution, the political upheavals which were foretold. The soil, they said, would pass into other hands; the harvests of foreign lands would come in and swamp our own; there would be nothing but brambles in our fields. Well, what of it? Have we the power to destroy the earth? Whatever happens, she'll belong to someone, and that someone will be forced to cultivate her so as not to die of hunger. If weeds grow over her for years, she'll be rested, she'll regain her youth and her fertility. The earth takes no part in our maddened insect-struggles; she is the eternal worker, ceaselessly toiling and taking no more notice of us than a nest of ants.

There was grief too, and blood, and tears, all the things which make men suffer and rebel. Françoise was killed, Fouan killed, the wicked triumphant, the bloodthirsty stinking vermin of the villages polluting and preying upon the earth. But who can tell? Just as the frost that sears the crops, the hail that slashes them to shreds, the lightning that smashes them down, are all, maybe, necessary things, so it might be that blood and tears were needed to make the world move on. What does our happiness count in the great system of the stars and the sun? God cares precious little about us! We only gain our bread through a terrible struggle renewed day after day. Only the earth remains immortal, our mother from whom we come and to whom we return, the earth that we love enough to do murder for her. She uses even our crimes and our miseries to make life and more life for her hidden ends.

For a long time this confused daydream whirled cloudily through his brain. But a trumpet sounded in the distance, the trumpet announcing the arrival of the Bazoches fire-engine galloping up too late. When he heard it, he suddenly straightened himself. It seemed like war passing amid clouds of smoke, with its horses and cannons and bloodthirsty cries. His heart beat loudly. Well, as he no longer had the heart to till the soil of France, he'd defend it in battle!

He turned to go, but looked for one last time at the two bare earth-mounds of the graves, and then beyond them to the endless ploughlands of La Beauce, filled with the unceasing gesture of sowing. Death and the sowing of seeds: and the life of bread growing up out of the earth.
Earth, Part V, ch. vi

It is true that Zola maintains in this passage a pretence of realistic objectivity by appearing to recount nothing more than what is going on in the mind of his central character. But it is evident to anyone who knows him that he is expressing through Jean some of his own deepest and most enduring feelings and convictions about nature, life, death, the problem of evil, and human destiny.

Epical genius

Zola's genius is not only lyrical; it is also epical, as we may see above all in *Germinal*. In this novel, which is almost universally admired today as one of the greatest masterpieces of modern literature, he realised his youthful dream to write an epic—not (as he had written in a youthful letter to a friend) just another stupid imitation of the classics—but an original epic on such contemporary themes as modern man's hopes for the future and his revolutionary longing for liberty. Among the book's most celebrated passages are those depicting the march of a hungry mob of strikers across a frozen plain. In the first of the following two excerpts, we see them through the generally sympathetic eyes of the author; in the second, they are portrayed as they appear to a group of fearful bourgeois who have taken refuge in a barn.

II

Under a pale wintry sun the mob straggled off across the bare frosty plain, spilling over the edges of the road, trampling down the fields of beet.

From the Fourche-aux-Boeufs Etienne had taken over

control. Without calling a halt, he shouted orders and organised the march. Jeanlin ran on in front, blowing outlandish music on his horn. Next came the women in the front ranks, some of them armed with sticks, Maheude wild-eyed, as though she were gazing into the distance for the coming of the promised city of justice, Ma Brûlé, la Levaque, Mouquette, striding along in their rags like soldiers marching off to the war. If they ran into any trouble they would see whether the troops would dare to strike women. After them the straggling herd of men formed a spreading tail, bristling with crowbars, over which stood out the single axe of Levaque, with its edge gleaming in the sunlight. Etienne, in the middle, kept an eye on Chaval whom he forced to march in front of him, whilst Maheude from further back cast disapproving glances at Catherine, who was the only woman amongst all these men, determined to run along near her lover so that they could not hurt him. They were bareheaded, with tousled hair, and no sound could be heard but the clatter of clogs, like the trampling of cattle turned loose and driven on by Jeanlin's wild trumpetings.

Suddenly a new cry rang out:

'We want bread! We want bread!'

It was midday, and the hunger of a six-weeks' strike, intensified by this march across country, was growing acute in their empty bellies. The few crusts of the morning, Mouquette's chestnuts, were now things of the distant past, their stomachs were crying out for food and their suffering put the finishing touch to their fury against the traitors.

'To the pits! Stop all work! We want bread!'

Germinal, Part V, ch. iv

12

'Courage!' he said. 'We'll sell our lives dearly.'

This witticism only increased their alarm. The noise was coming nearer; so far nothing could be seen, but a wind seemed to sweep the empty road, like a sudden squall preceding a great storm.

'No, no, I don't want to look,' said Cécile, cowering down in the hay.

Madame Hennebeau looked very pale. She was irritated at these people coming and spoiling one of her pleasures, and was standing well back, casting sidelong glances of disapproval, but Lucie and Jeanne, although trembling, had their eyes glued to a crack, for they were anxious not to miss any of the show.

The thunder drew nearer, shaking the very earth, and then Jeanlin was the first to appear, running along and blowing his horn.

'Get out your smelling-salts, the sweat of the people is going by,' murmured Négrel who, for all his republican convictions, liked to laugh at the common people when he was with ladies.

But his witty remark was lost in the din of the shouting and gesticulating mob. The women had come into sight, nearly a thousand of them, dishevelled after their tramp, in rags through which could be seen their naked flesh worn out with bearing children doomed to starve. Some of them had babies in their arms and raised them aloft and waved them like flags of grief and vengeance. Others, younger, with chests thrown out like warriors, were brandishing sticks, whilst the old crones made a horrible sight as they yelled so hard that the strings in their skinny necks looked ready to snap. The men brought up the rear: two thousand raving madmen, pit-boys, colliers, repairers in a solid phalanx moving in a single block, so closely packed together that neither their faded trousers nor their ragged jerseys could be picked out from the uniform earth coloured mass. All that could be seen was their blazing eyes and the black holes of their mouths singing the *Marseillaise*, the verses of which merged into a confused roar accompanied by the clatter of clogs on the hard ground Above their heads an axe rose straight up amidst the bristling crowbars, a single axe, the banner of the mob, and it stood out against the clear sky like the blade of the guillotine.

'What dreadful faces!' was all Madame Hennebeau could find to say.

Négrel muttered :

'Devil take me if I can recognise a single one! Where have all these ruffians come from?'

And indeed rage, hunger, and two months of suffering, and then this wild stampede through the pits, had lengthened the placid features of the Montsou miners into something resembling the jaws of wild beasts. The last red rays of the setting sun bathed the plain in blood, and the road seemed like a river of blood as men and women, bespattered like butchers in a slaughterhouse, galloped on and on.

'Oh, how wonderful!' whispered Lucie and Jeanne, whose artistic taste was deeply stirred by the lovely horror of it all.

Nevertheless they were afraid and fell back towards Madame Hennebeau, who was leaning for support against a trough. She was appalled as she realised that one glimpse through the cracks in this rickety door would suffice, and they would all be slaughtered. Even Négrel, usually so brave, felt himself grow pale with a fear stronger than his will-power, the fear of the unkown. Cécile continued to lie motionless in the hay. As for the others, try as they might to avert their gaze they could not do so, but went on looking.

And what they saw was a red vision of the coming revolution that would inevitably carry them all off one bloody night at the end of this epoch. Yes, one night the people would break loose and hurtle like this along the roads, dripping with bourgeois blood, waving severed heads and scattering gold from rifled safes. The women would yell and the men's teeth would be bared like the jaws of wolves ready to bite. Yes, it would be just like this, with the same rags, the same thunderous trampling of heavy clogs, the same dreadful rabble with filthy bodies and stinking breath, sweeping away the old world like the onrush of a barbaric horde. Fires would blaze and not a single stone would be left standing in the cities, and after the great orgy, the grand feast, when in a single night the poor would empty the cellars of the rich and rip open their women, nothing would be left but wild life in the forests. Nothing at all: not a sou of anybody's wealth, not one title-deed of any established fortune, pending the day when a new world would be born, perhaps. Yes, this was what was passing them by along the road like a force of nature, they could feel its deadly blast blowing in their faces.

Over and above the *Marseillaise* a great cry went up: 'We want bread! We want bread!'

Germinal, Part V, ch. v

What gives these and similar passages in the novel their epic quality is not just, of course, the subject matter, which is epic enough, but also the powerful poetic imagination of the author. His dramatic sense, his narrative skill, his gift for significant exaggeration, his ability to invest an action based on specific historical events with universal significance, his brilliant use of imagery transform the scenes he describes into poetic visions worthy of the greatest epic poets of the past. We may note, among other things, his use of repetition, his mastery of the art of portraying crowds, his symbolic use of the colour red (one of the two dominant colours of the book), and above all, perhaps, the art with which, by a kind of epic explosion, he turns his coal miners into archetypes of all the world's hungry and oppressed.

Nightmare

Zola's novels contain numerous passages as nightmarish as anything in Kafka's fiction or Goya's paintings. In *Thérèse Raquin*, for example, the scar from a bite made on a murderer's neck by his victim takes on a frightening life of its own.

13

His most acute suffering, both physical and moral, came from the bite on his neck made by Camille. There were times when he imagined that this scar covered the whole of his body. If he did happen to forget the past, the stinging pain he seemed to feel brought the murder back to his body and mind. He could not stand in front of a mirror without seeing the phenomenon he had so often noticed before but which frightened him still: under the stress of his emotion the blood rose to his neck and inflamed the wound, which began to itch. This wound living on him, so to speak, waking up, reddening, and biting him at the slightest upset, was a cause of dread and torture to him. He came to fancy that the drowning man's teeth had implanted some creature there which was gnawing at him.

43

The part of his neck where the scar was seemed to have ceased to belong to his own body, but was like some stranger's flesh grafted on, a piece of poisoned meat rotting his own muscles. Wherever he went he carried with him a living and devouring reminder of his crime. Whenever he hit Thérèse she tried to scratch him on the place, and sometimes she dug her nails in and made him scream with pain. Usually she pretended to cry when she caught sight of the bite, so as to make it still more unbearable for him. Her whole revenge for his ill-treatment of her consisted in torturing him by means of this bite.

Many times while shaving he had been tempted to cut his neck and obliterate the tooth-marks. When he raised his chin and saw in the glass the red mark showing through the lather, he flew into sudden tempers and jabbed with the razor as if to cut right into the flesh. But the cold steel on his skin always brought him back to himself, and then he felt faint and had to sit down and wait for his cowardliness to settle down and let him finish shaving.

Thérèse Raquin (1867), ch. xxx

Symbolic expression of our age

Freudian critics have found in Zola's fiction considerable evidence of his own private phobias and obsessions. Yet his art, like all great art, is much more than an expression of the personal peculiarities of its creator. It is to a very high degree symptomatic and symbolic of the age in which we live and the whole spirit of our times. This is evident throughout his work, but nowhere more so than in the following description of the death of a horse and the flight of two young lovers through the galleries of the flooded mine in *Germinal*.

14

Progress was very slow because the water was now up to their chests. So long as they had a light they would not despair, and so they put out one of the lamps in order to save oil, intending to empty it into the other. As they reached the chimney, a noise behind them made them turn. Had the others also been cut off and forced back this way? There was a distant sound of stentorian breathing, like an approaching storm lashing the water into foam. For a moment they were mystified, then they uttered a scream of terror as a gigantic whitish mass loomed up out of the darkness, fighting its way towards them through the narrow timbers between which it was nearly jammed.

It was Bataille. On leaving pit bottom he had galloped along the black galleries, panic-stricken, but still sure of his way in this underground city where he had lived for eleven years, for his eyes could see quite clearly through the eternal night in which he had spent his life. On and on he galloped, lowering his head, lifting his feet, speeding through these narrow warrens where his great body could only just pass. Roads followed roads and junctions forked this way and that, but he never hesitated. Where was he bound? Over yonder, maybe, towards that dream of his youth, that mill on the Scarpe where he was born, that distant memory of the sun burning up there like a big lamp. He wanted to live, his animal memories came back to him; a longing to breathe once again in the air of the plain carried him on, straight on, in the hope of that hole which led out into the light of day under the warm sky. His lifelong resignation was swept away in a fierce revolt against this pit that had first blinded him and now was trying to kill him. The water was pursuing him: now it was lashing his thighs, now licking his rump. But as he plunged onward the galleries narrowed and the roofs came lower, the walls jutted out. Nevertheless he galloped on, grazing his flanks and leaving his bleeding flesh on the jagged timbers. The mine was pressing in on him from every side: it was going to get him and crush the life out of him.

As he came nearer, Catherine and Etienne saw him wedge himself finally between the rocks. In stumbling he had broken both his forelegs. With one last effort he dragged himself a few metres along, but his haunches would not pass through, and there he was, snared and garrotted by the earth. He craned forward his bleeding head, still looking for some crack with his great frightened eyes. The water was rapidly rising over him, and he began to whinney, with the same long-drawn-out, agonised cry with

46

which the other horses had perished in the stable. It was a fearful death; this poor old animal, mutilated, held prisoner, was struggling his last struggle in the bowels of the earth, so far from the light of day. His cry of distress never stopped, and even when the flood reached his mane it still went on, only more raucous, as his mouth stretched upwards, wide open. Then there was a final snoring sound, and a muffled gurgling like a barrel being filled. Then silence.

'Oh, God! take me away!' sobbed Catherine. 'Oh, God. I'm frightened, I don't want to die. Take me away!'

She had looked on death. Neither the collapsing shaft nor the flooded pit had filled her with such horror as this death-cry of Bataille. It went on echoing in her ears and sent a shudder through her whole being.

'Take me away! Take me away!'

Etienne seized her and carried her off. It was high time, for they were in water up to their shoulders as they began to climb up the chimney. He had to help her up, for she had no strength left to hold on to the timbers. Three times he thought he was going to drop her into the deep, swirling waters below. They were able to stop for a few minutes' breathing space when they reached the first level, where it was still dry. But the water caught them up, and they had to hoist themselves still higher. And so the climb went on for hours as the flood drove them from level to level, always forcing them upwards. At the sixth there was a respite which filled them with excitement and hope, for the water seemed to remain stationary. But then it rose more quickly than before, and they had to climb to the seventh, and then to the eighth. There was only one more left, and when they reached that they anxiously watched every centimetre that the water rose. Unless it stopped, was this to be their death, crushed against the roof with water filling up their lungs—like the old horse?

At every moment some new fall re-echoed. The whole mine was convulsed, for its entrails were too weak to hold all this liquid on which the creature was gorged, and they were bursting. Pockets of air, compressed into blind galleries, went off in terrible detonations, splitting the rocks and overthrowing great blocks of earth. This terrifying din of internal cataclysms was like those prehistoric upheavals when deluges turned the earth inside out, burying the mountains under the plains.

Germinal, Part VII, ch. v

Undoubtedly there are reflections here of more than one of Zola's eccentricities; e.g., his fear of tunnels. But the whole passage also expresses in images of great symbolic power certain preoccupations, attitudes, and intuitions characteristic of many other modern artists. One may think, for example, of Picasso's *Guernica*. Both the writer and the painter depict events that occurred or presumably occurred during the bitter final stages of revolutionary conflicts. Both portray scenes of panic in which the pain and terror of the human victims are shared and symbolised by animals. Both represent figures trapped in dark, confining spaces. Both contain solar images. Both show women holding lamps. But in addition to these, and other perhaps somewhat fortuitous resemblances, both betray to a high degree the fascination of the modern artist with the theme of violence. Both go far beyond a simple realistic depiction of particular historical events to make very similar statements about the human condition in general. Both, like so many other modern artists, verge on the apocalyptic. Both strike much the same modern note of horror, fear, and anguish.

Premonitions of disaster

The world Zola describes in his major novels is a world shaken by catastrophe and threatened by even greater upheavals to come. The destruction of the mine in *Germinal*, the runaway train full of singing soldiers in *The Beast in Man*, the concluding episodes of the Franco-Prussian War and the Paris Commune in *The Downfall* turn into symbols of much more terrible disasters. The incident of the runaway train, for example, prefigures not only the infinitely graver misfortunes about to befall the France of Louis Napoleon during the war with Germany but also the truly fearful calamities that must necessarily result from technological progress in a civilisation which fails to achieve adequate control over the atavistic side of human nature.

15

Then, with a final effort, Pecqueux flung Jacques out, but just as Jacques felt space round him, in his desperation he succeeded in clutching at Pecqueux's neck, so convulsively that he dragged his murderer down with him. A double wild cry, voices of murderer and murdered confused in one, broke against the wind and was dispersed into nothingness. They fell together and as these two men, who so long had been like two brothers, went down, the draught of the train drew them in under the wheels, to be cut up, chopped into pieces, still laced together in a terrible embrace. Their bodies were afterwards found headless, legless, two bleeding trunks, with arms still enlaced one about the other, in suffocating grasp.

Devoid of control, the locomotive continued its wild rush through the night. At last this frisky, self-willed young thing, like a young, unbroken mare escaping from her rider, could indulge all the unchecked frenzy of her adolescence and gallop at will across the open land. The boiler was topped with water, the fire-box was roaring wildly, full of coal, and for the next half hour pressure rose madly and the speed became terrifying. The guard must have fallen asleep, worn out with fatigue, no doubt. And as being herded together body to body like that made the wine go to the soldiers' heads still more, this wild plunge of the train at reckless speed made them crazy with excitement and they yelled their songs at the top of their voices. They swept through Maromme at lightning speed, but their whistle no longer sounded as they came up to signals or rushed through stations. It was the all-out gallop of a maddened wild animal which rushes, head down, blindly at any obstacle. On and on rushed locomotive 608, as if the stridency of her own infuriated breathing made her yet madder still.

At Rouen they were supposed to halt to take in water, and the station hands were aghast when between the platforms they saw her flash through in dizzy whirl of smoke, a train insane, a locomotive without either driver or fireman, and eighteen cattle-trucks cram-full of soldiers yelling patriotic ditties. They were going crazily to the war. This speed was merely to bring them more quickly to the shores of the Rhine. The men in the stations they passed through gaped and waved their arms. The general alarm went up. Out of all control, this runaway train would never get through Sotteville without meeting some obstacle, Sotteville was always in the throes of shunting, waggons and locomotives all over the place, for Sotteville was one of France's railway towns. And they rushed to the telegraph to warn Sotteville, just in time to have a goods train on the track shunted to a siding. Men were everywhere waiting for it, and, ears alert, caught its roar before it came near. Twice, outside Rouen, it plunged into tunnels, twice it emerged again, at wild gallop, a terrible, uncheckable force which nothing now could stop. Like wildfire it reached Sotteville, and without harm roared its path among obstacles to plunge again, a roar gradually receding, on into darkness.

By now the telegraph was busy all down the line. Hearts pounded with alarm when men heard the news of this ghost train seen flying through Rouen, through Sotteville, towards Paris. There was general fear. In front of it ran the regular express, into which this mad thing would crash. Like a wild boar through the forest it swept on its course, regardless of fog signals or red signal lights. At Oisel it all but crashed into a shunting engine. Its speed apparently undiminished, it terrified Pont-de-l'Arche. And again it vanished into the night, rushing on and on, no man knew whither.

What matter the victims which that locomotive might crush in its tracks! Was it not itself plunging on into the future? So why care about blood spilt? Driverless in the darkness, blind, deaf beast let loose among death, on it rushed, packed to the full with cannon-flesh, with soldiers now stupid with fatigue, in drunken song.

The Beast in Man (1890), ch. xii

Awareness of world destruction and renewal

No writer has more powerfully expressed the awareness of modern man that he is living in what the Greeks would have called a time ripe for a new metamorphosis of the gods. In *The Downfall*, for example, the French defeat of 1870 and the tragic events of the Commune are made to symbolise the spiritual death and resurrection of the nation and suggest in the process an almost Nietzschean philosophy of history. This is particularly evident in the book's final pages, where Jean Macquart, now a soldier, is shown brooding over a fallen comrade.

16

. . . Oh, what a way to go, with a whole world crashing down around you! On the last day, now that it was all over, and the Commune was dying in the midst of all these fresh ruins, what was the use of still another sacrifice! He had gone from life, hungering for justice, in the supreme throes of the great, sombre dream that had possessed him, that grandiose, monstrous conception of the old society destroyed, Paris burned, the field ploughed up once again so that from the renewed and purified soil might spring the idyl of a new golden age.

Jean, his heart full of anguish, turned around and looked at Paris. It was a beautiful, clear Sunday evening, the setting sun on the horizon flooded the immense city with its fiery light. It looked like a sun of blood upon a shoreless sea. Thousands of windows had been turned by it into embers shimmering as if blown by invisible bellows; the roofs glowed like beds of live coals; fragments of yellowed walls and tall, rust-coloured monuments flashed and sparkled like burning brushwood in the evening air. It was the final pyrotechnic display, the gerb reserved for the grand finale of the imperial celebration, the gigantic bouquet of purple as if all of Paris were burning like a giant bundle of sticks, some tinder dry primaeval forest soaring heavenward in a great cloud of sparks and swarming flames. The fires were still raging, vast volumes of reddish smoke were still rising, and you could hear a loud murmur coming from the distance, perhaps the last death-rattles of the Communists they had shot at the Lobau barracks, or perhaps it was the rejoicing of the women and the laughter of the children who had seemed to be having such a good time roaming through the streets and who were now sitting eating their suppers like happy picnickers, on the front steps of the wine-shops. In the midst of all these ransacked buildings, these torn-up pavements, all this suffering and ruin, you could still hear life going on, yes, even as this flaming star sank in royal splendour, and Paris, like a vast holocaust, appeared to crumble into ashes.

Then Jean had an extraordinary sensation. It seemed to him as he stood there watching the sun slowly setting over this city in flames, that a new day was already dawning. It was true that he was witnessing the end of everything, the workings of a relentless destiny, an accumulation of disasters unparalleled in the history of nations: the continual defeats, the provinces lost, the millions in indemnities, the most frightful civil war imaginable quenched in blood, whole quarters reduced to rubble and strewn with corpses, no more money, no more honour, the whole world to rebuild! And he thought brokenheartedly of his own terrible losses. A part of himself lay there, too, under the ruins, along with Maurice and his dream of a happy future married to Henriette. And yet, beyond this fiery furnace still roaring about him, Hope, the eternal, was being reborn in the depths of the vast, tranquil sky. It was the certain rejuvenation of an everlasting Nature, of an imperishable Humanity, the renewal promised to him who keeps on working and does not despair, the tree that throws out a new and vigorous shoot to replace the rotten branch that had to be chopped off because its blighted sap was causing the young leaves to wither and turn yellow. . . .

La Débâcle (1892), Part III, ch. viii

Prophetic bent

Not only *The Downfall*, but many of Zola's other works are strongly prophetic. *Germinal*, for example, is in large part a symbolic adumbration of the future. 'This novel,' he jotted down in his work notes, 'is the revolt of the proletariat, a rude shove given society, which cracks open for a second—in a word the conflict between capital and labour. That's precisely where the importance of the book lies : I want it to predict the future, to pose the question which will be the most important question of the 20th century.' It is, therefore, not surprising that this epic account of a major industrial strike in the last years of the Second Empire ends with an apocalyptic vision of greater struggles to come, followed by a new Golden Age.

17

Yes, Maheude was right when she said in her sensible way that that would be the big day, when they could legally band together, know what they were doing and work through their unions. Then, one morning, confident in their solidarity, millions of workers against a few thousand

EZ—E
55

idlers, they would take over power and be the masters. Ah, then indeed truth and justice would awake! Then that crouching, sated god, that monstrous idol hidden away in his secret tabernacle, gorged with the flesh of poor creatures who never even saw him, would instantly perish. . . . Deep down underfoot the picks were still obstinately hammering away. All his comrades were there, he could hear them following his every step. Beneath this field of beet was it not Maheude, bent double at her task. whose hoarse gasps for breath were coming up to him, mingled with the whirring of the ventilator? To left and to right far away into the distance he thought he could recognise other friends under the corn, the hedges, and young trees. The April sun was now well up in the sky, shedding its glorious warming rays on the teeming earth. Life was springing from her fertile womb, buds were bursting into leaf and the fields were quickening with fresh green grass. Everywhere seeds were swelling and lengthening, cracking open the plain in their upward thrust for warmth and light. The sap was rising in abundance with whispering voices, the germs of life were opening with a kiss. On and on, ever more insistently, his comrades were tapping, as though they too were rising through the ground. On this youthful morning, in the fiery rays of the sun, the whole country was alive with this sound. Men were springing up, a black avenging host was slowly germinating in the furrows, thrusting upwards for the harvest of future ages. And very soon their germination would crack the earth asunder.

Germinal, Part VII, ch. vi

Unanimism

In 1885, shortly after the publication of *Germinal*, Zola wrote the great French critic Jules Lemaître:

I am quite willing to accept your definition of my work: 'A pessimistic epic of human animality'—but on the one condition that you let me explain what I mean by the word *animality*. You identify man with his brain; I put him in all his organs. You isolate man from nature; I cannot envisage him apart from the earth, from which he comes and into which he returns. The soul that you lock up within the individual creature I feel to be present everywhere, inside the individual and outside, in his brother the animal, in the plant, in the stone.

The following passage is typical of many others in Zola's works where he illustrates this philosophical view of nature by showing all the elements of creation vibrating with a single life, a single soul, a single purpose.

18

It was the garden that had planned and willed it all. For

weeks and weeks it had been favouring and encouraging their passion, and at last, on that supreme day, it had lured them to that spot, and now it became the Tempter whose every voice spoke of love. From the flower-beds, amid the fragrance of the languid blossoms, was wafted a soft sighing, which told of the weddings of the roses, the love-joys of the violets. . . . And the forest proclaimed the mighty passion of the oaks. Through the high branches sounded solemn music, organ strains like the nuptial marches of the ashes and the birches, the hornbeams and the planes, while from the bushes and the young coppices arose noisy mirth like that of youthful lovers chasing one another over banks and into hollows amid much crackling and snapping of branches. From afar, too, the faint breeze wafted the sounds of the rocks splitting in their passion beneath the burning heat, while near them the spiky plants loved in a tragic fashion of their own, unrefreshed by the neighbouring springs, which themselves glowed with the love of the passionate sun.

'What do they say?' asked Serge, half swooning, as Albine pressed him to her bosom. The voices of the Paradou were growing yet more distinct. The animals, in their turn, joined in the universal song of nature. The grasshoppers grew faint with the passion of their chants; the butterflies scattered kisses with their beating wings. The amorous sparrows flew to their mates; the rivers rippled over the loves of the fishes; whilst in the depths of the forest the nightingales sent forth pearly, voluptuous notes, and the stags bellowed their love aloud. Reptiles and insects, every species of invisible life, every atom of matter, the earth itself joined in the great chorus. It was the chorus of love and of nature—the chorus of the whole wide world; and in the very sky the clouds were radiant with rapture, as to those two children Love revealed the Eternity of Life.

Abbé Mouret's Transgression, Part II, ch. xv

Lofty view of man

The portraits that Zola has left us of his nineteenth-century French contemporaries are frequently so brutal and sombre that one is sometimes tempted to accuse him of maligning the human race. Nevertheless there are indications in his works that, far from having an unreservedly low opinion of mankind, he is quite as capable as many other great moralists of viewing man as an essentially noble creature —even in his present tragic state of degradation. One may think, for example, of his highly symbolic account of the death of Little Charles, the youngest of the Rougons, while Tante Dide, the ancient matriarch of the Rougon-Macquart family, watches helplessly. The event takes place in an asylum. The old woman is insane. The boy is an imbecile —an extreme case of hereditary degeneracy. But Zola portrays him as an angelically beautiful child dressed like a little prince and, at the beginning of the episode, has him cutting out paper pictures of soldiers, captains and 'kings, arrayed in purple and gold'. Then, as he bleeds to death, he shows him with his cheek resting on these royal images.

19

. . . When he was left alone with Tante Dide he resumed

his cutting out very quietly. This continued for a quarter of an hour in the profound silence of the asylum in which only distant sounds, reminiscent of a prison, could be heard; a furtive footstep, the clinking of a bunch of keys, then, sometimes, wild cries, immediately muffled. But on this torrid day the child must have felt tired and he dozed off. Soon his head, lily-white, nodded under the heavy helmet of his royal crown of hair; then it dropped, gently, on top of the pictures, he was sound asleep, one cheek resting on the purple and gold of the kings. His eye-lashes shadowed the other cheek, life ran feebly through the little blue veins under his fragile skin. He was as beautiful as an angel, with the undefinable corruption of a whole race stamped on his countenance. And Tante Dide went on staring at him vacantly, with neither pleasure nor pain, as eternity might look if it stared at the earth.

But at the end of a few minutes her clear eyes showed a faint glimmer of excitement. Something had happened, a red drop was swelling at the tip of the child's left nostril. The drop fell, and another gathered and followed it. It was blood spouting like red dew, noiselessly, with nothing to account for it, no blow this time; it came out of its own accord and dripped away, the sign of degeneration. The drops coalesced to make a thin flow which dripped on to the gold of the pictures. Soon they were obliterated by a pool which spread towards the corner of the table; then the drops gathered more quickly, ran into each other and dropped heavily on to the tiles of the floor. And still he slept on, looking like a divinely calm cherub, without any idea that his life was escaping from him; and the madwoman went on staring at him, looking more excited but with no sign of fear, diverted if anything, her eye caught by the bright colour as it would have been by big flies, the flight of which she often followed for hours.

Doctor Pascal (1893), ch. ix

Concern with ultimate principles

The following two passages, both from *Doctor Pascal*, are excellent examples of Zola's strong tendency, observable throughout his writings, to aspire after an all-embracing vision of the cosmos. They may also be used to illustrate his lifelong struggle with the problem of evil, his exalted faith in life, and his belief, as deep as that of Voltaire, in the value of hard work.

20

. . . There is no absolute evil. There has never been a man who is all bad, the worst of men is capable of conferring happiness on someone; with the result that, if one avoids a rigidly unitary point of view, one ends up by realising that every man has his uses. Those who believe in a God should say to themselves that, if God does not strike down the wicked, it is because he sees his creation as a whole, and does not descend to the particular. All labour finishes and starts again; it is impossible to avoid admiring the courage and indefatigability of mankind; and the love of life is stronger than anything. This gigantic labour of man, this clinging to life, is its excuse, its redemption. Thus, from a high vantage point, one would see nothing but this continual struggle, and much good, in spite of all the evil. One became infinitely indulgent, one pardoned, one was filled with overwhelming pity. This is surely the haven, awaiting all those who have lost faith in dogmas, who want to understand why they are alive, amidst the apparent iniquity of the world. To live for the sake of the struggle, to add one stone to the distant and mysterious edifice, and the only joy possible on this earth is the joy of sustained effort.

Doctor Pascal, ch. v

21

. . . Life from its vantage point of eternity was not afraid to create one more life. It pursued its purpose, indifferent to all hypotheses, propagating itself according to its own laws, ever marching forward with infinite labour. Its mission was to create, go on creating, even at the risk of creating monsters, because, in spite of the maimed and the mad, there was always the hope that, in the end, it would create a new healthier and wiser race. Life was like an enormous river, flowing endlessly towards its unknown objective! Life was never still, tossing us to and fro, with its currents and counter-currents, like an immense and boundless sea!

Doctor Pascal, ch. xiv

Utopian and messianic tendencies

If Zola's earlier novels show us primarily the world as it is, those he wrote towards the end of his life show us the world as he wants it to be, a world redeemed by human industry, the beneficent workings of an ever-fruitful nature, and the force of truth and justice. The following extracts are highly characteristic of this later, predominantly visionary Zola.

22

. . . Life is the rising tide whose waves daily continue the work of creation, and perfect the work of awaited happiness, which shall come when the times are accomplished. The flux and reflux of nations are but periods of the forward march : the great centuries of light, which dark ages at times replace, simply mark the phases of that march. Another step forward is ever taken, a little more of the earth is conquered, a little more life is brought into play. The law seems to lie in a double phenomenon; fruitfulness creating civilisation, and civilisation restraining fruitfulness. And equilibrium will come from it all on the day when the earth, being entirely inhabited, cleared, and utilised, shall at last have accomplished its destiny. And the divine dream, the generous utopian thought soars into the

heavens; families blended into nations, nations blended into
mankind, one sole brotherly people making of the world
one sole city of peace and truth and justice! Ah! may eternal fruitfulness ever expand, may the seed of humanity
be carried over the frontiers, peopling the untilled deserts
afar, and increasing mankind through the coming centuries
until dawns the reign of sovereign life, mistress at last both
of time and of space!

Fruitfulness (1899), Book VI, ch. v

23

. . . Outside, under the window, the children were happily
playing. You could hear the chatter of the littlest ones and
the laughter of the older ones; it was a foretaste of the happiness awaiting the race, as it marched towards the future.
The great blue sky was over them, and the beneficent sun,
the father and fertiliser, whose fire had been stolen and
turned to domestic uses, was shining on the horizon. And
under its glorious rays the roofs of Beauclair sparkled
triumphantly—at this time of day a bee-hive of active
workers whom, now that labour had been reformed and re-
generated, were happy because there was a just division
of wealth among them.

Work (1901), Book III, ch. v

24

. . . Some had dared to say, 'Happy the poor in spirit!' and
from that mortal error had sprung the misery of two thousand years. The legend of the benefits of ignorance now
appeared like a prolonged social crime. Poverty, dirt, super-
stition, falsehood, tyranny, woman exploited and held in
contempt, man stupefied and mastered, every physical and
every moral ill, were the fruits of that ignorance which had
been fostered intentionally, which had served as a system
of state politics and religious police. Knowledge alone

64

would slay mendacious dogmas, disperse those who traded and lived on them, and become the source of wealth, whether in respect to the harvests of the soil or the general florescence of the human mind. No! happiness had never had its abode in ignorance; it lay in knowledge, which will change the frightful field of material and moral wretchedness into a vast and fruitful expanse, whose wealth from year to year culture will increase tenfold.

Thus Marc, laden with years and glory, had enjoyed the great reward of living long enough to see his work's result. Justice resides in truth alone, and there is no happiness apart from justice. And after the creation of families, after the foundation of the cities of just work, the nation itself was constituted on the day when, by decreeing integral education for all its citizens, it showed itself capable of practising truth and equity.

Truth (1903), Book IV, ch. iv

Part Two: The Realist

Emphasis on true detail

Zola once said that he loved to come across pages of 'frightening truth', and it is precisely this awesome truth-fulness that he achieves in his greatest novels. One of the ways he does so is through the accumulation of small, harsh facts, which he presents to the reader without comment, leaving him free to form his own conclusions. This description of an apartment house in the Paris slums is a good example.

25

They had passed through the arched doorway and crossed the courtyard. The Lorilleux lived on the sixth floor, stair-case B. Coupeau laughingly told Gervaise to hold the hand-rail tight and not to leave go of it. She looked up, and blinked on perceiving the lofty well of the staircase, which was lighted by three gas-jets, one on every second landing; the last one, right atop, looking like a star twinkling in a black sky, whilst the other two cast long beams of light, of fantastic shapes, among the interminable windings of the stairs.

'Hallo!' said the zinc-worker, as he reached the first floor landing, 'there's a strong smell of onion soup. Some one's been having onion soup, I'm sure.'

As a matter of fact the grey, dirty B staircase, with its greasy hand-rail and stairs, and scratched walls showing the rough mortar, was still full of a powerful odour of cooking. On each landing passages branched off sonorous with noise, and yellow painted doors, blackened near the locks by dirty hands, stood open; while, on a level with the staircase window, a musty stench came from the drain-sink mingling with the pungency of the cooked onions. From the ground-floor to the sixth storey one could hear the clatter of crockery, the noise of saucepans being scoured, of pans being scraped with spoons to clean them. On the first floor, where a door, bearing in big letters the inscription 'Draughtsman,' stood ajar, Gervaise caught sight of two men conversing angrily amidst the smoke from their pipes, whilst seated at an oilcloth covered table, whence the evening meal had just been cleared away. The second and third floors were quieter; through the chinks of the woodwork one merely heard the rocking of a cradle, the smothered cries of a child, and the full voice of a woman, all intermingling and flowing on like the dull murmur of a stream, without any one word being distinctly audible. And Gervaise read different names on placards nailed upon the doors: 'Madame Gaudron, carder,' for instance; and farther off: 'M. Madinier, manufactory of cardboard boxes.' People were fighting on the fourth floor, which shook with the stamping of feet and upsetting of furniture, accompanied by an awful noise of oaths and blows; all this, however, did not prevent the neighbours across the landing from playing cards, with their door open, so as to get a little air.

When Gervaise reached the fifth floor, she stopped to draw breath; she was not used to so much climbing; that ever turning wall, and the glimpses of lodgings which she caught in fast succession, made her head ache. Besides, a family now blocked up the landing; the father was washing some plates in a pan on a little earthenware stove near the sink, whilst the mother, leaning against the hand-rail, was washing the baby before putting it to bed. However, Coupeau encouraged the young woman. They were nearly there, said he; and when he at length reached the sixth landing, he turned round to aid her with a smile. She, with raised head, was trying to discover whence came a clear, piercing voice, dominating all other noises, which she had heard from the first stair. It came, she found, from an attic under the roof, where a little old woman was singing as she dressed some cheap dolls. Then, as a tall girl entered a room close by with a pail of water, Gervaise espied a man inside, and when the door had been closed, she read upon a card nailed to it: 'Mademoiselle Clémence, ironer.' And now, right at the top of the stairs as she was, short of breath, and with her legs exhausted, she had the curiosity to lean over the hand-rail. At present it was the lowest gas-jet which looked like a star at the bottom of the narrow well by which the six flights descended; and all the odours and turbulent, seething life of the house came up in one breath, as it were, to the spot where she stood, scorching her anxious face as with a gust of heat, as she paused on the edge of the abyss.

But Coupeau spoke: 'We're not there yet,' said he. 'Oh! it's quite a journey!'

L'Assommoir (1877), ch. ii

Such buildings, of course, actually exist, but even if we did not wish to believe this it would be difficult to do so; Zola's details are too convincing. It is hard to see how he could have imagined them. And he does not simply tell us that this sort of establishment may be found in the working-class quarters of Paris; he *shows* one to us, he appeals directly to our senses. We smell the onion soup,

68

hear the woman's heavy voice flowing on like the dull murmur of running water, see the gaslight flickering at the bottom of the narrow stair well, feel the hot air rushing up, and share Gervaise's dizziness and fatigue as she reaches the top.

Historical authenticity

Zola went to enormous lengths to verify the historical details in his novels, but, occasionally, he exercised the
novelist's prerogative to sacrifice absolute veracity in the
interests of dramatic effect or—what was more important
—higher truth. For example, it has never been absolutely
determined whether or not Louis Napoleon actually wore
rouge to conceal his pallor when he appeared before his
troops before the battle of Sedan. But it was poetically
right that the man who personified the decadent Second
Empire with all its theatrical sham should go down to
defeat made up like an actor. To those who accused Zola
of demeaning the Emperor by representing him as a buf-
foon, he retorted, 'I myself find this paint a superb detail,
worthy of one of Shakespeare's heroes, imparting heightened nobility to the figure of Napoleon III by adding to it
a certain tragic, infinitely grandiose melancholy.'

26

Was not that the Emperor and his staff? He hesitated to
answer the query affirmatively, although, since he had
70

almost spoken to Napoleon at Baybel, he had flattered himself he should at once recognise him anywhere. Then he suddenly opened his mouth and looked on gaping. Yes, it was indeed Napoleon III, to all appearance taller now that he was on horseback, and with his moustaches so carefully waxed, and his cheeks so highly coloured that Delaherche immediately came to the conclusion that he had sought to make himself look young again—in a word, that he had made himself up for the occasion like an actor. Ay, without doubt he had caused his valet to paint his face so that he might not appear among his troops spreading discouragement and fright around him with his pale, haggard countenance distorted by suffering, his contracted nose, and dim, bleared eyes. And warned, at five o'clock, that there was fighting going on at Bazeilles, he had set out thither, silent and mournful like a phantom, but with his cheeks all aglow with rouge.

On the way some brickworks afforded a shelter. The walls on one side were being riddled by the bullets raining upon them; and shells were at every moment falling on the road. The entire escort halted.

'It is really dangerous, sire,' said some one; but the Emperor turned round, and with a wave of the hand simply ordered his staff to draw up in a narrow lane skirting the works, where both men and horses would be completely hidden. 'It's really madness, sire—we beg you, sire—'

However, he simply repeated his gesture, as though to say that the appearance of a number of uniforms on that bare road would certainly attract the attention of the hostile batteries on the left bank of the Meuse. And then, all alone, he rode forward amid the bullets and the shells, without evincing any haste, but still and ever in the same mournful, indifferent manner, as though he were going in search of Destiny. And doubtless, he could hear behind him that implacable voice that had ever urged him forward, the voice that rang out from Paris, calling: 'March, march, die like a hero on the corpses of your people, strike the whole universe with compassionate admiration, so that your son may reign!'

The Downfall, Part II, ch. i

Concern with general truths

The characters, settings, and situations in Zola's novels are almost all meant to represent the larger wholes of which they are a part and to suggest general truths about them. The following passage, for example, derives much of its realism from the depressing truth it is intended to convey about the treatment of the poor—even by some representatives of the clergy.

27

The beadle was waiting for them in the middle of the empty church; and pushed them towards a little side chapel while asking them angrily whether it was to show their contempt for religion that they arrived so late. A sulky-looking priest, whose face was pale with hunger, then advanced with great strides, preceded by an acolyte trotting along in a dirty surplice. The reverend gentleman hurried through the mass, gobbling up the Latin phrases, turning about, stooping, spreading out his arms, all in great haste, whilst glancing askance at the bridal couple and their witnesses. In front of the altar, Coupeau and Gervaise, feeling very ill at ease, not knowing when they ought to kneel, stand up or

73

sit down, waited for signs from the acolyte. The witnesses, in order to be decent, stood up the whole time, whilst Mother Coupeau, again overcome by tears, wept into the open missal which she had borrowed from a neighbour. However, twelve o'clock had struck, the last mass had been said, and the church gradually resounded with the tread of the sacristans' footsteps and the noise of chairs being put back in their places. The high altar was evidently being got ready for some grand religious ceremony, for one could hear the hammering of upholsterers who were nailing up the hangings. And in the depths of the little out-of-the-way chapel, amidst the dust raised by the beadle, who was sweeping around, the sulky-looking priest quickly passed his bony hands over the bent heads of Gervaise and Coupeau, whom he seemed to be uniting in the midst of a removal. When the wedding party had again signed a register in the vestry, and were once more out in the sunshine beneath the porch, they remained there for a moment, bewildered and out of breath at having been despatched so quickly.

L'Assommoir, ch. iii

Conformation with scientific theory

Zola believed that novelists could achieve heightened truth by incorporating into their works the latest scientific theories. In practice, however, he often seems more anxious to appeal to the popular cult of science than to impress those who are truly scientifically minded. The following passage is a good example of pseudo-scientific melodrama if there ever was one!

28

'Look out,' snarled Chaval. 'This time I'm going to get you!'

Then Etienne went mad. A red mist swam before his eyes and blood surged up to his head. The blood-lust was upon him, as imperious as a physical need, as a lump of phlegm in the throat that makes you cough. It rose up in him and his will-power was swept away before the onrush of his hereditary taint. He laid hold of a flake of shale in the wall, tugged it from side to side until it came away. Huge and heavy though it was he raised it in both hands, and with superhuman strength brought it down on Chaval's skull.

He did not even have time to jump back, but went down with his face smashed in and skull split open. His brains spattered the gallery roof and a red flood streamed like a steady flowing spring, making a pool which reflected the smoky flame of the lamp. Darker shadows seemed to invade the narrow enclosed space, and the black corpse on the ground looked like a heap of slack.

Etienne stood over him, staring with dilated eyes. So he had done it, he had killed a man! All his past struggles swam through his consciousness; the unavailing fight against the latent poison in his system, the slowly accumulated alcohol in his blood. And yet he was far from drunk now, unless it were with hunger. The drunkenness of his parents long ago had sufficed. Though his hair stood on end at the horror of this murder, though all his upbringing cried out in protest, his heart was beating faster with sheer joy, the animal joy of an appetite satisfied at last.

Germinal, Part VII, ch. v

One may well ask if Zola ever really intended this to be a serious illustration of the quickly outmoded theories of heredity upon which it was presumably based. Is it not more likely that, like today's science-fiction writers, he was killing two birds with one stone—appealing to popular scientism while satisfying the public's thirst for fantasy and thrilling, violent action?

Emphasis on subjective appearances, point of view

Although Zola sometimes consulted photographs, he never set out to imitate the sort of objectivity that we associate with the camera. He not only defined art as 'a corner of nature seen through a temperament'; in his fiction he shows us a world filtered through multiple levels of consciousness —a world not of things in themselves, but of appearances. He seems to go out of his way, for example, to stress that the same sordid workers' dwelling that we have encountered in a previous extract does not seem ugly at all to Gervaise Macquart or to the poor children who live there.

29

. . . She did not think the house ugly. Amongst the rags hanging from the windows smiled various cheerful touches —a wall-flower blooming in a pot, a cage of canaries, whence a sound of chirruping descended, some shaving-glasses shining like stars in the depth of the shadow. Down below, a carpenter was singing, accompanied by the regular hiss of his jointing-plane; whilst, in the locksmith's workshop, a number of hammers beating in time sounded like a loud silvery peal of bells. Moreover, at almost all the open windows, against the faintly seen background of wretchedness, children showed their smeared and smiling faces, and women sewed, with placid profiles bent over their work. It was the resumption of toil after the mid-day meal, the rooms free of the men who worked away from home, the house relapsing into great peacefulness, on which only broke the noise of the workmen's tools, the lullaby as it were of a refrain, ever the same, repeated for hours together.

L'Assommoir, ch. ii

Similarly, he makes it a point to show the effects of distance. As seen from a remote prominence by the King of Prussia, the terrible battle of Sedan becomes a charming spectacle.

30

Somewhat tired, however, King William laid his field-glass aside for a moment, and continued examining the scene without its help. The sun was descending obliquely towards the woods, sinking to rest in a sky of unspotted purity; it gilded the whole vast stretch of country, bathed it in so limpid a light that the smallest objects acquired remarkable distinctness. The King could distinguish the houses of Sedan, with their little, black window bars, the ramparts and the fortress, all the complicated defensive works, clearly and sharply outlined. Then all around, scattered amid the fields, were the villages, fresh-coloured and shiny as with varnish, like the farmhouses one finds in boxes of toys. On the left was Donchery, at the edge of the level plain; on the right were Douzy and Carignan in the meadows. It seemed as though one could count the trees of the Forest of the Ardennes, whose sea of verdure stretched away to the frontier. In the crisp light, the lazily winding Meuse looked like a river of pure gold, and the fearful blood-smeared battle, seen from this height, under the sun's farewell rays, became as it were a delicate piece of painting. Some corpses of cavalry soldiers, and dead horses with their bellies ripped open, scattered bright touches over the plateau of Floing. Towards the right, in the direction of Givonne the eye was amused by the scrambles of the retreat, the vortex of running, falling black specks; whilst on the peninsula of Iges, on the left, a Bavarian battery, whose guns looked no bigger than lucifer matches, was served with such clock-work regularity, that it seemed like some piece of mechanism, carefully put together. And all this was victory—victory surpassing hope, overwhelming; and the King felt no remorse whatever as he looked down upon all those tiny corpses, those thousands of men occupying less space than the dust of the roads, that immense valley where neither the conflagrations of Bazeilles, the massacres of Illy nor the anguish of Sedan could prevent impassive nature from remaining beauteous in this, the serene close of a lovely day.

The Downfall, Part II, ch. vi

He also is interested in depicting things as they appear to people under intense strain. He notes, for example, at some length how, as Gervaise sinks lower and lower into poverty and vice, her own shadow assumes in her eyes a frightening nightmarish quality.

31

But suddenly she perceived her shadow on the ground. Whenever she came near to a gas-lamp it gradually drew itself together, became less vague, more clearly defined, and terribly grotesque, so portly had she nowadays grown. And such, moreover, was her lameness that the shadow seemed to turn a somersault at every step she took. It looked like a real Punch! Then as she left the lamp behind her, the

Punch grew taller, becoming in fact gigantic, filling the whole Boulevard, and bobbing to and fro in such a style that it seemed likely to smash its nose against the trees or the houses. Good heavens! how frightful she was! Never before had she realised her disfigurement so thoroughly. And from that moment she could not refrain from looking at her shadow; she even waited for the gas-lamps, ever watching the bobbing of that Punch-like reflection. Ah! she had a pretty companion with her! What a figure! It could scarcely be attractive! And at the thought of her unsightliness, she lowered her voice, and scarcely dared to stammer: 'Sir, just listen.'

L'Assommoir, ch. xii

And, finally, he is fascinated with the extreme forms of distortion that occur in hallucinations and dreams; e.g., a bad case of delirium tremens.

32

The doctor had now risen, and was listening to Coupeau, who in the full daylight was again troubled with visions of phantoms. He fancied that he saw cobwebs on the walls as big as the sails of ships! Then these cobwebs became nets, whose meshes grew smaller or larger, a queer sort of plaything! Black balls, too, passed in and out of the meshes, perfect juggler's balls, at first as small as marbles, and then as big as round shot; and they increased and they decreased in size, just with the object of bothering him. And all of a sudden, he exclaimed: 'Oh! the rats, there are the rats, now!'

L'Assommoir, ch. xiii

Delight in modern subjects

Zola's ideal of beauty, a man who knew him well once said, was a diamond in the shape of a locomotive. Like Baudelaire, he wanted to capture the peculiar essence of the modern world. How well he did so may be judged from this description of the impression made on a gateman's wife in her lonely cottage by the trains that regularly rumble past.

33

. . . and she found it queer to live lost like that, in the heart of a desert, without a soul to confide in, while day and night men and women were continually swept past her in a tornado of trains steaming all out and shaking her house as they passed. There was no doubt about it, the whole world went past her, not only French folk, foreigners too, folk from the most distant of lands, for nowadays nobody was capable of staying at home and, as someone had observed, all the peoples would soon blend into one. That was what progress was, men were all brothers, swept on all together on their swift wheels, on, on, into cloud-cuckoo-land. She made an attempt to tot them up, by average, at so many per coach. No, there were too many, it was beyond her. Frequently she thought she distinguished faces, among them that of a gentleman with a fair beard, who must be an Englishman. He went to Paris every week. And that of a dark little lady, who passed every Wednesday and Saturday. But the lightning flashed them by, she could never even be certain she had seen them at all, all those many faces melted together into one, commingling, merging one into the other, all alike. The torrent swept on, taking all with it. And what saddened her was feeling that despite such an incessant traffic of faces, all so well-off, with so much money displayed, that human multitude so passionately breathing did not even know of her existence there . . .

The Beast in Man, ch. ii

Emphasis on the power of environment

Like Gervaise in the following passage, Zola's characters are wholly submerged in their milieux, dominated and often ruthlessly assailed by *things*.

34

Behind her, the wash-house once more gave forth a great sluice-like noise. The women had eaten their bread and drunk their wine, and now they beat harder than ever, enlivened by the set-to between Gervaise and Virginie. All along the rows of tubs arms were again working furiously, whilst angular, puppet-like profiles, bent backs and distorted shoulders, kept jerking as though on hinges. Chattering continued along the different alleys, laughter and coarse remarks mingling with the gurgling sound of the water. The taps were running, the buckets over-flowing, and quite a little river streamed along beneath the washing-places. It was the moment of the afternoon's great effort, when the beetles fairly pounded the clothes. The vapour floating about the spacious building assumed a reddish hue, transpierced here and there by discs of sunshine, golden balls which found admittance through the holes in the blinds. And the atmosphere, laden with soapy odours, was lukewarm and stifling. Then suddenly the place became full of a white vapour. The huge lid of the copper where the lye was boiling rose mechanically on a central toothed rod, and from the gaping metal cavity set in brick-work came volumes of steam charged with the sweet savour of potash. Close by the wringers were in motion. Bundles of wet clothes, inserted between the cast-iron cylinders, yielded forth their water at one turn of the wheel of the panting, smoking machine, which shook the building more and more with the continuous working of its arms of steel.

When Gervaise set foot in the passage-entry of the Hôtel Boncoeur her tears again mastered her. It was a dark, narrow corridor, with a gutter for dirty water run-ning alongside one wall; and the stench which she again encountered there made her think of the fortnight she had passed in the place with Lantier—a fortnight of misery and quarrelling, the recollection of which was now fraught with bitter regret. It seemed as if she were plunging into abandonment.

Upstairs the room was bare, and full of sunshine, for the window stood open. That blaze of light, that dancing golden dust emphasised the wretchedness of the blackened ceiling and dirty walls, whose paper was half torn away. The only thing left hanging there—from a nail above the chimney piece—was a woman's small neckerchief, twisted like a piece of string. The children's bedstead had been drawn into the middle of the room, allowing a full view of the chest of drawers, the latter standing open and revealing all their emptiness. Lantier had washed himself and used the very last of the pomatum—a penn'orth of pomatum on a playing card; the greasy water from his hands still filled the basin. And he had forgotten nothing. The corner hitherto filled by the trunk seemed to Gervaise an immense empty space. Even the little hand-glass which hung from the window-fastening was gone. When she made this discovery she had a presentiment, and glanced at the mantelpiece. Lantier had taken away the pawn-tickets; the pink bundle was no longer lying there between the odd zinc candlesticks.

She hung her washing on the back of a chair, and remained standing, turning round and examining the furniture, overcome by such stupor that her tears could no longer flow. One sou alone remained to her of the four which she had kept for the wash-house. Then, on hearing Claude and Etienne, who already felt consoled, laughing at the window, she went up to them, mother like, took their heads under her arms, and for an instant forgot everything as she gazed on that grey highway, where she had beheld in the morning the awakening of the toilers, the dawn of the giant labour of Paris. At this hour the pavement, warmed by all the work of the day, sent a scorching reverberation up above the city, behind the octroi wall. It was on that pavement, in that furnace-like atmosphere, that she was cast all alone with her little ones; and her eyes wandered up and down the outer Boulevards, to the right and to the left, pausing at either end as covert terror fell upon her, as though her life would henceforth lie within those limits—a slaughter-house and a hospital.

L'Assommoir, ch. i

Note how the washerwomen are compared to marionettes, while machines assume tyrannical life, and the smell of slop water and the heat pouring up from the pavement violently assault Gervaise's senses. Note also how Zola focuses our attention on little things—a man's shaving mirror, pawn tickets, Gervaise's small savings—and stresses the important part that they play in the lives of his characters. We are very far indeed here from the abstract heroes and heroines, the bucolic, elegant shepherds and shepherdesses, the mythological Greek and Roman kings and queens of classical French fiction and drama who would seem to be able to exist independently of any particular setting.

Descent into the depths

Although Zola wrote about all levels of society and was quite capable of composing fiction in a light and happy vein, his best works are those which explore the cruel, sordid side of modern life—and do so without flinching, like a surgeon's scalpel probing a wound. His account of Gervaise's last days is a famous example.

35

In this wise Gervaise lasted for several months. She fell lower and lower still, submitting to the grossest outrages, and dying of starvation a little more every day. As soon as ever she had a few sous, she drank and fought the walls. M. Marescot had decided to turn her out of her room on the sixth floor. But, as old Bru was just about that time found dead in his hole under the staircase, the landlord kindly allowed her to turn into it. And now she roosted there in the place of old Bru. It was there, on some old straw, that she lay with chattering teeth, empty stomach, and frozen bones. Mother Earth would not have her apparently. She became idiotic, and did not even think of making an end of herself by jumping from a sixth floor window on to the pavement of the courtyard. Death was to take her little by little, bit by bit, dragging her thus to the bitter end through all the accursed existence that she had made for herself. And indeed it was never exactly known what she did die of. There was some talk of a cold; but the truth was she died of privation, of the filth and hardships of her wrecked life. According to the Lorilleux she simply rotted away. One morning, as there was a bad smell in the passage, it was remembered that she had not been seen for two days past, and she was discovered already mortifying in her hole.

L'Assommoir, ch. xiii

Preoccupation with the beast in man

Zola loved animals, whom he thought of as the 'little brothers' of man; and, as if to stress their resemblances to us, he often gave them human traits. On the other hand, he went out of his way to stress the bestial side of human nature, as in the following passage, in which Jacques Lantier, Nana's brother, suddenly realises after murdering his mistress that he is emitting noises reminiscent of wild beasts.

36

Jacques was utterly astounded. First he heard hoarse animal breathing, the growling of the beast of prey, the roar of a lion, then calming down, discovered it was his own breath. So at last he had done it, at last he had satisfied himself, and killed. Yes, he had done it. His heart raced free with a strange delight, which buoyed him up in this absolute satisfaction of the longing he had known so long. The result was an unexpected gift of pride, a build-up of his male superiority. He had killed this woman, therefore he had possessed her as for so long now he had desired, with nothing held back, not even her absolute annihilation. She was no more and would never be for any other man.

The Beast in Man, ch. xi

Concern with social behaviour

Zola is a profound student of human nature, but he is less interested in exploring individual personalities than he is in defining types and in describing group behaviour. The following excerpt from his description of a miner's fair-day is famous.

37

They stayed until ten. Women kept coming in to find their men folk and take them home; droves of children tagged on behind, and mothers, giving up any pretence of delicacy, took out breasts that hung down like long, yellow sacks of oats, and smeared their chubby offspring with milk; whilst the children who could already walk, blown out with beer, crawled about on all fours under the tables and shamelessly relieved themselves. All round there was a rising tide of beer, widow Désir's barrels had all been broached, beer had rounded all paunches and was overflowing in all directions, from noses, eyes—and elsewhere. People were so blown out and higgledy-piggledy, that everybody's elbows or knees were sticking into his neighbour and everybody thought it great fun to feel his neighbour's elbows. All mouths were grinning from ear to ear in continuous laughter. The heat was like an oven and everybody was roasting; so they made themselves comfortable by laying bare their flesh, which appeared golden in the thick clouds of pipe smoke. The only nuisance was when you had to go outside; now and again a girl would get up, go to the other end, lift her skirt by the pump and come back. Underneath the paper chains the dancers could no longer see each other for sweat, and this encouraged pit-boys to catch hold of backsides at random and throw haul-age girls on their backs. But when a girl fell down with a man on top of her, the cornet drowned their fall with its frenzied tootlings and feet trampled all over them as though the dance itself had buried them alive.

Germinal, Part III ch. ii

Preoccupation with binding relationships

Throughout Zola's novels, larger entities—a market, a department store, a railroad, a city—take on a life of their own which is more than the sum of the lives of the individuals of which they are composed. Moreover, as in his descriptions of the friendship between the two soldiers Maurice and Jean, he shows that he is deeply aware of the bonds that unite men despite their differences.

38

Leaning heavily on Jean's arm, Maurice then allowed himself to be led away. Never had woman's arm brought such warmth as this to his heart. Now that everything was crumbling to the ground, amid this extreme misery, with death threatening him, he experienced a delicious sensation of comfort, on realising that there was yet one who loved him and succoured him; and perhaps also the idea that this heart which was wholly his was the heart of a man of simple mind, of a peasant but slightly removed from the soil, and who had once been so repugnant to him, now added an infinite sweetness to his feelings of gratitude. Was not this the fraternity of the earliest days of the world, the friendship that existed long before there was any culture, before there were any classes; the friendship of two men, linked together, bound up in one another in their mutual need of assistance, threatened as they were by inimical nature? He could hear his humanity beating in Jean's breast, and he even felt proud that his comrade was stronger than himself, that he succoured him and devoted himself to him; whilst Jean, on the other hand, without analysing his sensations, experienced a feeling of delight in shielding his young friend's refinement and intelligence —qualities that in himself had remained in a rudimentary state. Since the violent death of his wife, carried off in a fearful tragedy, he had thought himself without a heart, and he had sworn that he would have nothing more to do with those creatures who bring man so much suffering, even when their natures are not evil. And the mutual friendship of Jean and Maurice became to both of them, as it were, an expansion of their beings; they did not embrace, and yet, however dissimilar their natures, they were none the less closely united, so bound up in one another, as they tramped along that terrible road to Remilly, the one supporting the other, that they seemed to form but one being compounded of pity and suffering.

The Downfall, Part I, ch. vi

Interest in eternal human themes

In passages like this one the distinction, precarious at best, that critics traditionally have made between Zola's poetic and realistic sides utterly breaks down. Is this description of a mother's musings as she nurses her infant realism or poetry? Zola himself, in a letter to a friend, claimed that it was pure realism, because, as he wrote, there was nothing *idealistic* about it. Yet he had himself once maintained that one of the chief characteristics of poetry is its preoccupation with the great, obvious facts of life and the eternal human truths; and in this sense, if in no other, this passage is surely poetic. Clotilde, as she holds her baby, has thoughts that might occur to any mother.

39

Clotilde came back to the table and sat down with the baby on her knees. He was kicking and crying. She smiled at him as she unhooked her dress. She bared her small round breast. The baby attracted by the odour of the milk was greedily searching for the nipple. When she put it in his mouth he gave a little grunt of satisfaction and started sucking voraciously. At first he had grasped her breast in his hand, as if to establish his right of possession. Then, as the warm flood filled him with primitive sensual joy, his hand released the breast and he raised his arm straight up in the air like a flag. And the sight of him so vigorously drawing his nourishment from her brought an involuntary smile to Clotilde's face. For a few weeks after her confinement she had suffered much pain from cracked nipples; they were still sensitive, but this did not interfere with her satisfaction at being able to suckle him.

*　　*　　*

A distant blare of music startled Clotilde. She turned her head and looked at the countryside, so bright and golden in the slanting sun. Ah! yes, the ceremony, the stone they were laying over there! Then she became engrossed again in the baby and watched him gorging himself. She pulled up a stool to raise one knee and leaned one shoulder against the table. Languid and content, she felt that her milk, pure essence of her maternal love, was binding this precious new being ever more closely to her. The child was come, the redeemer perhaps. The bells had pealed. The Wise Kings set forth on their journey, followed by the peoples, all nature rejoicing and smiling at the infant in his swaddling-clothes. She, the mother, as he sucked life from her breast, was dreaming about the future. If she devoted her whole life to him and made him big and strong, what would he become? A scholar who would pass on the eternal truths, a captain who would add to the glory of his country, or a pastor who would still the passions and usher in the reign of justice? Her son would be incomparably handsome, good and powerful. He would be the expected Messiah; it is fortunate for humanity that all mothers have this pathetic faith, without it mankind would not have the ever-renascent strength to go on living. What would he be like, this child? She looked at him closely, who did he resemble? He had his father's forehead and eyes, something

94

of the elongated and massive shape of his head. He had her own rather small mouth and delicate chin. Then she realised, with a shiver of apprehension, that she was looking for traces of the others, those grisly antecedents, whose lives were summarised on the Tree beside her. Which, if any of them, would he take after? She soon felt reassured, thanks to her natural optimism. Besides, her master had inculcated her with his boundless faith in life. What matter the miseries, sufferings, and abominations! Health and vitality depended upon work, the power which fertilises and gives birth. Life was rounded off by the child, the object of love. When love culminated in a child, all hopes were justified, despite all the hidden sores, the black picture of human shame.

*   *   *

All Clotilde's perfervid maternal instinct was aroused by that voracious little mouth drinking insatiably. The nation had been conquered and brought low. Someone had to rebuild it, was it not possible that her boy was the one appointed for the purpose? He would carry out the great experiment, raise the walls again, lead man, still groping in the darkness, into the light of a new faith, build the city of justice in which work alone could ensure happiness. In these troubled times, men were waiting for a prophet. Or, perhaps, they were waiting for the Antichrist, the demon of devastation, the predicted beast who would cleanse the earth of the filth and corruption which defiled it. And life would continue in spite of everything. It might be necessary to wait patiently for thousands of years, until the other child, the enigma, the benefactor, appeared.

The baby had emptied the right breast; and as he was fuming with impatience Clotilde turned him around and gave him the left breast. As she felt his gluttonous gums close on her nipple, she could not help smiling once more.

Doctor Pascal, ch. xiv

Fusion of traditional styles

Although Zola is still customarily introduced in literary manuals as the leader of the French naturalist school, his most significant achievement as a writer may have relatively little to do with his most famous naturalist theories (which he often blithely ignored in practice). Indeed as Erich Auerbach points out in *Mimesis*, one of his most remarkable contributions was to have provided us with one of the most extreme instances that we have of the tendency of modern Western literature to mix humble and sublime subjects and styles. Among the passages cited by Auerbach is this bit of working-class dialogue from *Germinal*, a perfect example of great historical tragedy composed out of subject-matter that most classical or neo-classical authors would have thought fit only for low farce. (Maheu is a typical miner. Maheude is his wife, Bonnemort his father. Etienne, the young hero of the novel, is their boarder.)

40

'Lord bless you!' Maheu replied, 'of course if there were more money there would be more comfort. All the same, it's quite true that it doesn't do people any good to live all on top of each other. It always ends up with the men tight and the girls in the family way.'

That started them all off, and each threw in his word, while the fumes of the oil lamp mingled with the reek of fried onions. You worked like a beast of burden at a job that used in the olden days to be a punishment for convicts, more often than not you died in harness, and with all that you could not even have meat on the table at night. Of course you had food of a kind, you did eat, but so little that it was just enough to keep you suffering without dying out-right, weighed down by debts and hounded as though you had stolen the bread you ate. When Sunday came round you were only fit to sleep. The only pleasures in life were to get drunk or get your wife with a baby, and even then the beer made you too fat in the paunch, and when the child grew up he didn't care a bugger about you. No, life wasn't funny at all.

Then Maheude chimed in :

'You see, the worst of it is when you have to admit that it can't ever change. When you are young you think hap-piness will come later later on, and you hope for things; and then the same old poverty gets hold of you and you are caught up in it. . . . Now I don't wish anybody any harm, but there are times when the injustice of it makes me mad.'

In the ensuing silence they all breathed hard, with the uneasy feeling of being hemmed in. Only Grandpa Bonne-mort, if he was there, raised his eyebrows in surprise, for in his day people used not to make such a fuss : you were born in coal, you hacked away at the seam and didn't ask questions, but now there was something in the air that gave miners high and mighty ideas.

'Mustn't turn your nose up at anything,' he would mur-mur. 'A good beer is a good beer. The bosses are often swine, but there'll always be bosses, won't there? What's the good of racking your brains to try and make sense out of it?'

That would start Etienne off. What! wasn't the worker allowed to think for himself? That was exactly why things were going to change soon, because the worker was beginning to think now!

Germinal, Part III, ch. iii

Part Three: Zola's 'Lie'

Fusion of naturalistic and poetic modes

The beginning of *Germinal* is an excellent example of what Zola meant by his 'lie'—i.e., his distinctive mixture of realism and poetry. On the surface it is a realistic description of a man walking down a road on a black, wintry night, coming across a coal mine, and going up to a fire-bucket to warm his hands and enquire about a job. At the same time, however, it conjures up a sombre Dantesque vision full of symbolism.

41

On a pitch-black, starless night, a solitary man was trudging along the main road from Marchiennes to Montsou, ten kilometres of cobblestones running straight as a die across the bare plain between fields of beet. He could not even make out the black ground in front of him, and it was only the feel of the March wind blowing in great gusts like a storm at sea, but icy cold from sweeping over miles of marshes and bare earth, that gave him a sensation of limitless, flat horizons. There was not a single tree to darken the sky, and the cobbled highroad ran on with the straightness of a jetty through the swirling sea of black shadows.

The man had set out from Marchiennes at about two. He strode on, shivering in his threadbare cotton coat and corduroy trousers. He was having trouble with a little bundle done up in a check handkerchief, which he held against his ribs first with one elbow and then with the other, so as to keep both his hands deep in his pockets, for they were numb and raw from the lashing winds. Being out of work and homeless, he had only one thought in his mind, and that was the hope that the cold would get less intense when daylight came. He had been tramping like this for an hour and was within two kilometres of Montsou, when to his left he saw some red flares—three braziers apparently burning in mid-air. At first fear held him back, but the urge to warm his hands for a minute was too painful to resist.

The road ran into a cutting and the fires disappeared. To his right there was a fence, a sort of wall of heavy baulks of timber shutting off a railway track, while to his left there rose a grass bank with some sort of roofs on top, like a village with low gables all the same size. He walked on about two hundred paces and suddenly, as he rounded a bend, the lights reappeared quite close, yet still he could not make out why they were burning high up in the dark sky, like smoky moons. But his eye was caught by something else at ground level; it was the solid mass of a block of low buildings, surmounted by the silhouette of a factory chimney. Here and there a light showed through a grimy window, while outside five or six dismal lanterns were hanging on blackened timber-work which stood like a row of gigantic trestles. Out of this weird, smoke-black vision there came a single sound: the heavy, laboured panting of an unseen exhaust-pipe.

Then he realised that it was a pit. His nervousness returned: what was the good? there was sure not to be any work. Instead of making for the buildings, he decided to venture up the slag-heap where the three coal fires were burning in buckets to give light and warmth to the workers. The rippers must have worked late, for the waste was still

100

being brought up. He could now hear the labourers push-
ing their trains along the trestles and pick out moving
shadows emptying the tubs near each of the fires.

'Morning,' he said, going up to one of the fire-buckets.

The haulier, an old man in a mauve jersey and felt cap,
was standing with his back to the fire, while his big, cream-
coloured horse stood like a statue, waiting for the six tubs
he had pulled up to be emptied. The man at the tip, a lanky,
red-haired fellow, was in no hurry and looked half asleep
as his hand worked the lever. Up above, the icy wind re-
doubled its fury with great regular gusts like the strokes of
a scythe.

Germinal, Part I, ch. i

All the details are based on Zola's observations of actual
mining communities in the region around Anzin, near Bel-
gium. But even as he describes his realistic scene he transforms it. The plain is metamorphosed into a black sea
rising up and threatening to engulf the man walking into
it. The pit becomes a monster. As the man approaches it
the wind redoubles its fury with great regular gusts like
the strokes of a scythe. One's impression that one is being
introduced into some kind of underworld is reinforced
by the analogy between the fire-buckets and smoky moons.
Even the cream-coloured horse and the mine workers have
something fantastic and dreamlike about them. The horse
stands as still as a statue. As the wind shrieks about them
the men move slowly and mechanically, half asleep.

Some of the major metaphorical themes of the book are
introduced in the process: the theme of the mine-monster;
the analogy between an industrial strike and a great storm;
and the analogy between the mines and the classical underworld and Christian hell. The scene is painted, moreover,
in the two dominant symbolic colours of this work: red
and black. And need it be pointed out that this flat, frozen,

limitless plain with its swirling sea of black shadows, its rhythmically wailing winds, its starless sky, and murky red flames is *poetically* right for a novel which depicts through the dramatic frame of a strike the rise of the proletariat— an epic novel developing many of the same ancient epic themes as Milton, Dante, Virgil, and Homer, but in a distinctively modern form?

Relation between realistic subject matter and metaphor

Zola's metaphors tend to be somewhat different from ordinary metaphors. They are not mere embellishments, nor, very often, are they primarily intended to help describe something. On the contrary, one frequently suspects that realistic objects are important to Zola primarily as pretexts for introducing some particular image which he needs for some poetic reason. And once such images have been evoked, they tend to prolong their existence by attaching themselves to other objects, taking on a kind of independent life of their own, growing into symbols and allegories. One might take for example the serpent image that occurs several times in *Germinal*, notably in the principal descriptions of mine interiors at the beginning, middle and end of the novel.

42

On a siding a stationary train was slumbering like a long black serpent. The horse snorted . . .

Part I, ch. iii

43

She was even glad to have something to think about and take her mind off her troubles in this unexpected climb, this human serpent moving upwards, three men to each ladder, and so long that its head would reach daylight while its tail was still dragging across the sump.

Part V, ch. ii

44

How many hours went by like this? They could not have said. All he knew was that there in front of him the creeping black water had reappeared at the mouth of the chimney, as though the malignant beast were arching his back so as to reach them. At first it was only a thin trickle, like a sinuous, lengthening serpent, but it broadened into the back of a sinister, crawling animal, then it caught them up and soon the sleeping girl's feet were in the water.

Part VII, ch. v

Note how these images are combined in a definite progression paralleling the development of the larger dramatic plot. In Part I, which takes place before the strike breaks out, Zola evokes the image of a sleeping serpent. In Part V, where the full violence of the strike erupts, he evokes the image of a leaping serpent. Finally in Part VII, which recounts the disasters produced by the strike, he shows us a serpent that has at last caught up with its victims. And each time the image reappears it has grown more monstrous, more terrible. Obviously Zola is engaged in much more than a simple metaphorical description of a train of coal-carts, a queue of miners escaping up the ladders of a shaft, or flood waters creeping through the galleries of a mine; he is completing the poetic transformation of the subterranean setting of the novel into a symbol of the hell of modern labour by including in it a traditional image of evil; and among other things, he is converting this traditional symbol into—it would seem—an allegory of economic class warfare.

Furthermore, in this as well as an almost infinite number of other ways, the poet in Zola contrives to express himself through the realist without, however, entirely breaking the realistic illusion. As I suggested at the beginning of this volume, this is one of the main sources—if by no means the only source—of Zola's power; this extraordinary ability to satisfy the conflicting needs of our paradoxical era, torn between realism and legend, poetry and science. In his fiction scientific, mythopoeic, positivistic, and idealistic modes of exploring and representing experience are reconciled through Titanic effort into a kind of unity which is perhaps possible only in works of art. At one end of the scale, those who are attuned primarily to realism in literature can appreciate a novel like *Germinal* or *La Terre* as a gripping human document without ever suspecting to what a great extent it is informed by a poetic vision of man and nature. Those of us on the other hand, who have fallen under the spell of this vision and look for evidence of it, inevitably witness a strange sort of metamorphosis. What at first seemed to be predominantly the work of a realist becomes more and more obviously the creation of a profoundly poetic imagination. And we may be tempted to regard even Zola's realism as the invention of a poet and itself, perhaps in the last analysis, a form of poetry—one of the many masks that the eternal spirit of poetry has fashioned for itself in the course of the ages.

Reference list of Zola's works

EARLY NOVELS

Claude's Confession (*La Confession de Claude*), 1865, tr. by George
   D. Cox, Temple Co., London, 1888.
A Dead Woman's Wish (*Le Voeu d'une morte*), 1866, tr. by Count
   C. S. de Soissons, Stanley Paul & Co., London, 1928; David McKay
   Co., Philadelphia, 1928.
The Mysteries of Marseilles (*Les Mystères de Marseille*), 1867, tr.
   by E. A. Vizetelly, Hutchinson & Co., London, 1895.
Thérèse Raquin, 1867, tr. by L. W. Tancock, Penguin Books, Har-
   mondsworth, Middlesex and Baltimore, Md., 1962.
Madeleine Férat, 1868, tr. by Alec Brown, Elek Books, London, 1957;
   Citadel Press, New York, 1957.

Les Rougon-Macquart

The Fortune of the Rougons (*La Fortune des Rougon*), 1871, Vize-
   telly and Co., London, 1886.
The Kill (*La Curée*), 1872, tr. by A. Teixeira de Mattos, Elek Books,
   London, 1957; The Citadel Press, New York, 1957.
Savage Paris (*Le Ventre de Paris*), 1873, tr. by David Hughes and
   Marie-Jacqueline Mason, Elek Books. London, 1955; The Citadel
   Press, New York, 1955.
A Priest in the House (*La Conquête de Plassans*), 1874, tr. by Brian
   Rhys, Elek Books, London, 1957; The Citadel Press, New York,
   1957.
The Sinful Priest (*La Faute de l'abbé Mouret*), 1875, tr. by Alec
   Brown, Arrow Books. London, 1967. (Vizetelly translation used

in this book, *Abbé Mouret's Transgression*, Chatto & Windus, London, 1900, now out of print.)

His Excellency (*Son Excellence Eugène Rougon*), 1876, tr. by Alec Brown, Elek Books, London, 1958; Dufour Editions, Chester Springs, Pa., 1958.

L'Assommoir, 1877, tr. by Atwood H. Townsend, The New American Library of World Literature, New York, 1962.

A Love Affair (*Une Page d'amour*), 1878, tr. by Jean Stewart, Elek Books, London, 1957; The Citadel Press, New York, 1957.

Nana, 1880, tr. by Lowel Bair, Bantam Books, New York, 1964.

Restless House (*Pot-Bouille*), 1882, tr. by Percy Pinkerton, Elek Books, London, 1957; Farrar, Straus & Young, New York, 1953.

Ladies' Delight (*Au Bonheur des Dames*), 1883, tr. by April Fitz-lyon, Abelard-Schuman, London and New York, 1958.

Zest for Life (*La Joie de vivre*), 1884, tr. by Jean Stewart, Elek Books, London, 1955; Indiana University Press, Bloomington, Indiana, 1956.

Germinal (1885), tr. by L. W. Tancock, Penguin Books, London and New York, 1954.

The Masterpiece (*L'Oeuvre*), 1886, tr. by T. Walton, Elek Books, London and New York, 1950.

Earth (*La Terre*), 1887, tr. by Ann Lindsay, Elek Books, London and New York, 1954.

The Dream (*Le Rêve*), 1888, tr. by E. E. Chase, Chatto & Windus, London, 1893.

The Beast in Man (*La Bête humaine*), 1890, tr. by Alec Brown, Elek Books, London, 1956.

Money (*L'Argent*), 1891, tr. by E. A. Vizetelly, Chatto & Windus, London, 1894.

The Downfall (*La Débâcle*), 1892, tr. by E. A. Vizetelly, Chatto & Windus, London, 1892; and tr. by E. P. Robins, The Macmillan Co., New York, 1898.

Doctor Pascal (*Le Docteur Pascal*), 1893, tr. by Vladimir Kean, Elek Books, London, 1957; Dufour Editions, Chester Springs, Pa., 1958.

Les Rougon-Macquart, Histoire naturelle et sociale d'une famille sous le Second Empire, texte intégral établi, annoté et présenté par Armand Lanoux et Henri Mitterand, Bibliothèque de la Pléiade, Paris, 1967.

The Three Cities (*Les Trois Villes*)

Lourdes, 1894, tr. by E. A. Vizetelly, Chatto & Windus, London, 1894.

REFERENCE LIST OF ZOLA'S WORKS

Rome, 1896, tr. by E. A. Vizetelly, Chatto & Windus, London, 1896.
Paris, 1898, tr. by E. A. Vizetelly, Chatto & Windus, London, 1898.

The Four Gospels (Les Quatre Evangiles)

Fruitfulness (Fécondité), 1899, tr. by E. A. Vizetelly, Chatto & Windus, London, 1900.
Work (Travail) 1901, tr. by E. A. Vizetelly, Chatto & Windus, London, 1901.
Truth (Vérité), 1903, tr. by E. A. Vizetelly, Chatto & Windus, London, 1903.

SHORT STORIES

Stories for Ninon (Contes à Ninon), 1864.
Parisian Sketches (Esquisses Parisiennes), 1866.
More Stories for Ninon (Nouveaux Contes à Ninon), 1874.
The Attack on the Mill (L'Attaque du moulin in *Les Soirées de Médan)*, 1880.
The Journal of a Convalescent (Le Journal d'un Convalescent), published in the notes appended to the Bernouard edition of *La Faute de l'Abbé Mouret*.
Captain Burle (Le Capitaine Burle), 1882.
Naïs Micoulin, 1884.
Madame Sourdis, 1929.

A complete collection of Zola's short stories will be found in Volume IX of Henri Mitterand's edition of Zola's works (see below). Good English translations are sadly wanting. Lafcadio Hearn's *Stories from Emile Zola* (ed. Albert Mordell, Hokuseido Press, Tokyo, 1935) is out of print and for most readers difficult to obtain. So also are *A Soldier's Honour and Other Stories* (Vizetelly & Co., London, 1888), *The Jolly Parisiennes and Other Novelettes* (tr. by George D. Cox, T. B. Peterson & Brothers, Philadelphia, 1888), *The Attack on the Mill and Other Sketches of War* (tr. by E. A. Vizetelly, William Heinemann, London, 1892), *Stories for Ninon* (tr. by E. A. Vizetelly, W. Heinemann, London, 1895), *Jacques Damour, Madame Neigeon, Nantas, How We Die, The Coqueville Spree, The Attack on the Mill* (tr. by W. M. Foster Apthorp, Copeland & Day, Boston, 1895), and the editions of The Warren Press, N. Y., 1911 (*Death, The Flood, For a Night of Love*).

REFERENCE LIST OF ZOLA'S WORKS

PLAYS

Théâtre, 1878 (*Thérèse Raquin, Les Héritiers Rabourdin, Le Bouton de Rose*).

Poems to be Set to Music (*Poèmes lyriques*), Fasquelle, Paris, 1921. Six opera librettos written for the composer Alfred Bruneau.

The Heirs of Rabourdin, a translation by A. Teixeira de Mattos of *Les Héritiers Rabourdin*, may be found in the Independent Theatre Series of Plays, no. 3, 1893. A translation of *Thérèse Raquin* is included in *Seeds of Modern Drama*, Dell Publishing Co., New York, 1966.

CRITICAL AND POLEMICAL WORKS, JOURNALS

My Hatreds (*Mes Haines*), 1866.

The Experimental Novel and Other Essays (*Le Roman expérimental*), 1880, tr. by Belle M. Sherman, Haskell House, New York, 1964 (reprint of a work first published in 1894). See also *The Experimental Novel*, ed. with intro. by Maxwell Geismar, Harvest House, Montreal, 1964.

The Naturalist Novelists (*Les Romanciers naturalistes*), 1881.

Naturalism in the Theatre (*Le Naturalisme au théâtre*), 1881.

Our Playwrights (*Nos auteurs dramatiques*), 1881.

Literary Documents, Studies and Portraits (*Documents littéraires*), 1881.

A Campaign (*Une Campagne*), 1882.

New Campaign (*Nouvelle Campagne*), 1897.

The Republic on the March (*La République en marche. Chroniques parlementaires, 1870–71*), ed. J. Kayser, Fasquelle, Paris, 1956.

My Travels (*Mes Voyages. Lourdes. Rome*), travel notes ed. by R. Ternois, Fasquelle, Paris, 1958.

Salons, ed. F. W. J. Hemmings and R. J. Niess, Droz, Geneva, 1959.

Zola's Atelier (*L'Atelier de Zola. Textes de journaux 1865–1870*), ed. M. Kanes, Droz, Geneva, 1963.

Letters from Paris (*Lettres de Paris*), ed. P. A. Duncan and V. Erdely, Droz, Geneva, 1963. (Extracts from articles published in Russia, 1875–80.)

COMPLETE EDITIONS

Emile Zola: Oeuvres complètes, a complete edition of Zola's writings, in fifteen volumes (18,000 pages) is currently being published under the direction of Henri Mitterand by the Cercle du Livre Précieux, Paris. It will contain far more material than any collection of Zola's works now in existence, including that edited by Maurice Le Blond and issued by the Bernouard Press, 1928–9.

LETTERS

Volume XV of the new Mitterand edition of the *Oeuvres complètes* (see above) will include, in addition to letters already published, more than a thousand previously unpublished letters. Until it appears, the largest collection remains that of the Bernouard editon (see above), which contains about six hundred letters.

Select bibliography

SOME INVALUABLE SOURCES OF
BIBLIOGRAPHICAL INFORMATION

Les Cahiers naturalistes, a bi-annual review published by the
   Société Littéraire des Amis d'Emile Zola and Editions Fasquelle,
   Paris. Each issue lists all current European and American studies,
   including theses and work in progress, having to do with Zola,
   naturalism, and the Dreyfus Affair.
French VII, a bibliography of 20th century French Literature
   edited for the French Institute, 22 East 60th St., New York 22,
   N.Y. Each edition contains a list of books and articles on Zola
   published since the preceding edition.
HEMMINGS, F. W. J., *Emile Zola*, 2nd ed., The Clarendon Press,
   Oxford, 1966. Includes a bibliography of the principal documen-
   tary sources of our knowledge of Zola's life, together with a
   large selection of the more useful books and articles that have
   been written about his work.
—— 'Zola par delà la Manche et l'Atlantique (essai bibliographi-
   que)', *Les Cahiers naturalistes*, 23 (1963), 299–312. A list of books
   and articles on Zola published from 1953 through 1962, accompanied by brief summaries and descriptions.
MITTERAND, HENRI and SUWALA, HALINA, *Bibliographie chronologi-
   que et analytique des articles d'Emile Zola (1859–1881)*, Les
   Belles-Lettres, Paris (Annales de la Faculté des Lettres et Sciences
   Humaines de Besançon), 1968.
MLA International Bibliography, published annually in *PMLA*,
   journal of the Modern Language Association of America. A
   major bibliography compiled from a master list of about 1,150

periodicals, and from various book sources. Lists books and articles written in English, French, German, and other languages.

The Year's Work in Modern Language Studies, a major annual bibliography edited for the Modern Humanities Research Association. Includes brief descriptions and judgments of works listed.

ZOLA, E., *Oeuvres complètes*, 15 vols., Cercle du Livre Précieux, Paris, 1966. Contains bibliographical references in the notes preceding each work.

—— *Les Rougon-Macquart*, 5 vols., Gallimard, Bibliothèque de la Pléiade, Paris 1960–67. A valuable bibliography is included in the notes for each novel.

USEFUL STUDIES OF ZOLA'S LIFE AND WORK

The following list includes the principal biographies of Zola and a selection of books and articles on those aspects of his life and work of greatest interest to contemporary readers.

ÅHNEBRINK, L., *The Beginnings of Naturalism in American Fiction*, Harvard University Press, Cambridge, Mass., 1950. Includes a detailed study of Zola's influence on Hamlin Garland, Stephen Crane, and Frank Norris.

ALEXIS, P., *Emile Zola, notes d'un ami*, Charpentier, Paris, 1882. An illuminating biography by one of Zola's closest friends and disciples. Its description of Zola's method of composition, however, is somewhat misleading.

AUERBACH, E., *Mimesis, The Representation of Reality in Western Literature*, tr. by W. R. Trask, Princeton University Press, Princeton, N.J., Oxford University Press, London. 1953. (Zola, 506–15.) An attempt by a brilliant scholar to define Zola's place in the general European literary tradition.

BÉDÉ, J. A., *Emile Zola*, Columbia University Press, New York (Columbia Essays on Modern Writers), 1968. A succinct, informative introduction to Zola's life and works.

BROMBERT, V., *The Intellectual Hero, Studies in the French Novel, 1880–1895*, Lippincott, Philadelphia and New York, 1961. ('The apostolate of Marc Froment', 68–9.) According to Mr. Brombert, Marc Froment, the hero of *Truth*, 'is an intellectual who, nevertheless, lacks the temperament of an intellectual'.

BROWN, C. S., *Repetition in Zola's Novels*, University of Georgia Press, Athens, Georgia, 1952. A study of Zola's use of repetition, one of his most important devices.

BURNS, C. A., 'Documentation et imagination chez Emile Zola',

Les Cahiers Naturalistes, nos. 24–5 (1963), 69–78. An essay offering interesting insights into Zola's creative use of documents.

CARTER, L. A., *Zola and the Theater*, Yale University Press, New Haven, Conn., 1963. A study of the development of Zola's naturalist theories, his plays, librettos, dramatic criticism, collaborations; stage adaptations of his works; and other playwrights of the same epoch.

CITRON, P., 'Quelques aspects de la création littéraire dans l'oeuvre d'Emile Zola', *Les Cahiers Naturalistes*, nos. 24–5 (1963), 47–54. A study of Zola's portrayal of Paris in the first nine *Rougon-Macquart* novels.

COGNY, P., 'Emile Zola devant le problème de Jesus-Christ d'après des documents inédits', *Studi Francesi*, viii (1964), 255–64. An article shedding new light on Zola's value as a religious thinker.

CORNELL, K., 'Zola's City', *Yale French Studies*, No. 32 (1964), 106–11. An essay on Zola's portrayal of Paris by a major authority on the French Symbolist movement.

DECKER, C. R., 'Zola's literary reputation in England', *PMLA*, xlix (1934), 1140–54. A study of the English reaction to Zola.

DOUCET, F., *L'Esthétique d'Emile Zola et son application à la critique*, De Nederlandsche Boek- en Steendrukkerij 1923. A Somewhat superficial but still valuable analysis of Zola's aesthetic theories, critical writings and artistic practice.

DUBOIS, J., 'Les Refuges de Gervaise. Pour un décor symbolique de *l'Assommoir*', *Les Cahiers Naturalistes*, No. 30 (1965), 105–17. A delicate study of the symbolic aspects of the setting of *L'Assommoir*.

DUNCAN, P., 'Zola's machine monsters', *Romance Notes*, iii (1962), 1–3. Mr. Duncan points out a certain ambivalence in Zola's attitude towards technology and the machine.

FRANDON, I. M.. *Autour de 'Germinal'. La Mine et les mineurs*, Droz, Geneva, 1955. A scholarly study of the sources and genesis of *Germinal*.

FRANZÉN, N. O., *Zola et 'la Joie de vivre'. Genèse du roman, les personnages, les idées*, Champion, Paris, 1958. A scholarly study of the genesis of *La Joie de vivre*.

GIRARD, M., 'Naturalisme et symbolisme', *Cahiers de l'Association internationale des études françaises*, no. 6, (1954), 97–106. A study of Zola's relations with the symbolists and symbolist aspects of his own works.

—— 'L'univers de *Germinal*', *Revue des Sciences humaines*, fasc. 69 (1953), 59–76. A brilliant exploration of the poetic, visionary side of *Germinal*.

—— 'Zola visionnaire', Montjoie, i (1953), 6–9. An essay on Zola's visionary qualities.

GRANT, E. M., 'The composition of *La Curée*', *Romanic Review*, xlv (1954), 29–44. Description and analysis of Zola's work notes for *La Curée*.

—— *Emile Zola*, Twayne Publishers, New York, 1966. A concise, scholarly, readable introduction to Zola's life and works.

—— *Zola's 'Germinal'. A Critical and Historical Study*, Leicester University Press, 1962. A useful, scholarly work designed to meet the needs of the student or teacher of Zola's masterpiece, bringing together the results of previous scholarship and supplementing and completing it with additional research. Although the poetic aspects of the novel are discussed in some detail, it is appreciated primarily for its realism.

GRANT, R. B., *Zola's 'Son Excellence Eugène Rougon'*. Duke University Press, Durham, N. C., 1960. A scholarly study of the background, sources, genesis, and composition of *Son Excellence* together with an appraisal of Zola's art in this novel.

GUILLEMIN, H., *Présentation des 'Rougon-Macquart'*, Gallimard, Paris, 1964. A scholarly but deeply personal exploration of Zola, with particular emphasis on his treatment of money, sex, politics, and religion.

HAMILTON, G. H., *Manet and his Critics*, Yale University Press, New Haven, 1954. Includes (81–111) a chapter on Zola and Manet.

HEMMINGS, F. W. J., 'The Elaboration of Character in the *Ebauches* of Zola's *Rougon-Macquart* Novels', *PMLA*, lxxxi (1966), 286–96. A study of Zola's creative procedures, particularly in respect of the invention, modification, and elaboration of his fictional characters in the *Ebauches* (preliminary outlines) of his novels.

—— *Emile Zola* (see above). The principal work on Zola in the English language. The revised edition, like the first, examines and evaluates Zola's works in chronological order against the background of his life.

—— & Niess, R. J. *Emile Zola. Salons*, Droz, Geneva, 1959. A collection of Zola's articles on art, with an interesting introduction by Hemmings.

—— 'The origin of the terms *naturalisme, naturaliste*', *French Studies*, viii (1954), 109–21. Concludes that Zola probably borrowed the term *naturaliste* from Taine, while the term *naturalisme* was first repeatedly employed by Belinski, in an important article on Russian literature published in 1848.

JAGMETTI, A., *'La Bête humaine' d' Emile Zola, étude de stylistique critique*, Droz, Geneva, 1955. An exploration of the poetic symbolism and structure of *La Bête humaine*.

KANES, M., 'Zola and Busnach : the temptation of the stage', *PMLA*, lxxvii (1962), 109–15. This study of Zola's collaboration with

Busnach and the latter's theatrical adaptations sheds new light on Zola's dramatic theories.

—— Zola's 'La bête humaine'. A Study in Literary Creation. Univ. of Calif. Press, Berkeley, 1962. A valuable genetic study.

LANOUX, A., *Bonjour, Monsieur Zola*, Amiot-Dumont, Paris, 1954. A popular, very readable biography.

LAPP, J. C., 'The watcher betrayed and the fatal woman: some recurring patterns in Zola', *PMLA*, lxxiv (1959), 276–84. A study of certain obsessions of Zola's, expressed throughout his novels in recurrent scenes and situations.

—— *Zola before the 'Rougon-Macquart'*, University of Toronto Press, Toronto, 1964. A stimulating examination of Zola's early short stories and novels which places Zola in the novelistic tradition stretching from the 18th century to the present and provides certain valuable insights into his mature work.

LE BLOND-ZOLA, D., *Emile Zola raconté par sa fille*, Fasquelle, Paris, 1931. An informative biography by Zola's daughter.

LEVIN, H., *The Gates of Horn: a Study of Five French Realists*, Oxford University Press, New York, 1963. Contains a stimulating study of Zola (305–71).

LUKÁCS, G., *Studies in European Realism*, Hillway Publishing Co., London, 1950. An often cited Marxist view of Zola ('The Zola centenary', 85–96).

MALLARMÉ, S., *Dix-neuf lettres de Stéphane Mallarmé à Emile Zola*, Centaine, Paris, 1929. Letters to Zola by the great symbolist poet, who was one of Zola's most faithful friends and admirers.

MASSIS, H., *Comment Emile Zola composait ses romans*, Fasquelle, Paris, 1906. An important early study of Zola's method of composition particularly with respect to *L'Assommoir*.

MATTHEWS, J. H., 'The art of description in Zola's *Germinal*', *Symposium*, xvi (1962), 267–74. A study of how Zola expresses his determinism in description of the setting.

—— *Les Deux Zola*, Droz, Geneva, 1957. A detailed investigation of ways objective and subjective elements are combined in Zola's style.

—— 'Things in the naturalist novel', *French Studies*, xiv (1960), 212–23. The role of *things* in Zola's novels.

—— 'Zola and the Marxists', *Symposium*, xi (1957), 262–72. A summary of some Marxist judgments of Zola (Paul Lafargue, George Lukács, Jean Fréville, and others).

MAX, S., *Les Métamorphoses de la grande ville dans les 'Rougon-Macquart'*, A. G. Nizet, Paris, 1966. A perceptive analysis of Zola's poetic vision as seen in his portrayal of Paris.

MITTERAND, H., 'Quelques aspects de la création littéraire dans l'oeuvre d'Emile Zola', *Les Cahiers naturalistes*, nos. 24–5 (1963), 9–20. Brilliant insights into Zola's creative imagination and method of composition by a leading French authority on Zola

—— 'Thérèse Raquin' au théâtre', *Revue des Sciences humaines*, fasc. 104 (1961), 489–516. About the theatrical version of Thérèse Raquin.

—— *Zola journaliste. De l'affaire Manet à l'affaire Dreyfus*, Armand Colin, Paris, 1962. An informative history of Zola's career as a journalist with numerous excerpts from his articles, chronological tables, a list of Parisian journals and their featured critics during the years 1864–6, a table showing the circulation of Parisian dailies in December 1865 and October 1868, and a bibliography of Zola's articles in *Mes haines* and other collections with original dates of publication.

—— Notes, Variantes et Index, Emile Zola, *Les Rougon-Macquart*, 5 vols., Gallimard, Bibliothèque de la Pléiade, Paris, 1967. Mitterand's notes treating the sources, genesis, publication, and critical reception of each novel, are of extreme value and must be consulted by anyone contemplating serious work on Zola.

NIESS, R. J., *Zola, Cézanne, and Manet: A Study of L'Oeuvre*, Univ. of Mich. Press, Ann Arbor, 1968. A thorough study of *L'Oeuvre*, assessing eighty years of critical thought.

PATTERSON, J. G., *A Zola Dictionary*: with a Biographical and Critical Introduction, Synopses of the Plots of the *Rougon-Macquart* Novels, and a Bibliographical Note, Routledge, London, 1912. Still a useful compendium.

PEYRE, H., Introduction, Emile Zola, *Nana*, Collier Books, New York, 1962. An introduction by a great authority on French literature.

PICON, G., 'Le "réalisme" d'Emile Zola: du "tel quel" à l'oeuvre objet', *Les Cahiers naturalistes*, 22 (1962), 235–40. Insights into the nature of Zola's 'realism' by a major contemporary French critic.

PROULX, A., *Aspects épiques des Rougon-Macquart de Zola*, Mouton, The Hague, 1966. A revealing study of Zola's epic side.

PSICHARI, H., *Anatomie d'un chef-d'oeuvre: 'Germinal'*, Mercure de France, Paris, 1964. A re-examination of Zola's portrayal of his Montsou miners in the light of present knowledge about the French working class during the second half of the 19th century.

REWALD, J., *Paul Cézanne: a Biography*, Simon & Schuster, New York, 1948. English version of *Cézanne, sa vie, son oeuvre, son amité pour Zola*, Albin Michel, Paris, 1939, which has a larger bibliography. Contains a great deal of information about Zola's friendship with Cézanne

ROBERT, G., *Emile Zola. Principes et caractères généraux de son oeuvre*, Les Belles Lettres, Paris, 1952. An introduction to Zola, with which every student should be familiar.

—— '*La Terre*' *d'Emile Zola, étude historique et critique*, Les Belles Lettres, Paris, 1952. A remarkably profound and scholarly study of the background, sources, genesis, subject matter, art, and impact of *La Terre*.

—— 'Zola et le classicisme', *Revue des Sciences humaines*, fasc. 49 (1948), 181–207, and fasc. 50 (1948), 126–53. A study of Zola's curiously ambivalent attitude towards the classical tradition, acquaintance with specific classical writers, debt to the classics, affinities with the classics, etc.

RUFENER, H. L., *Biography of a War Novel, Zola's 'La Débâcle'*, King's Crown Press, New York, 1946. A genetic study of *La Débâcle*.

SALVAN, A. J., *Zola aux Etats-Unis*, Brown University Press, Providence, R. I., 1943. A history of Zola's literary reputation in the United States.

TANCOCK, L. W., 'Some early critical work of Emile Zola : *Livres d'aujourd'hui et de demain* (1866)', *Modern Language Review*, xlii (1947), 43–57. A pioneering study.

TERNOIS, RÉNÉ, 'La Naissance de *l'Oeuvre*', *Les Cahiers naturalistes*, 17 (1961), 1–9. An article shedding light on the origins of *L'Oeuvre*.

—— 'Le stoïcisme d'Emile Zola', *Les Cahiers naturalistes*, 23 (1963), 289–98. An analysis of a certain 'stoicism' in Zola's thought and attitudes, influenced by Taine and Guyau and growing logically out of his positivism and naturalism.

—— *Zola et son temps. Lourdes—Rome—Paris*, Les Belles Lettres, Paris, 1961. A complex, many-sided, fascinating book growing out of the author's desire to present Zola's trilogy, *Les Trois Villes* in the light of the period which they reflect.

TOULOUSE, E., *Enquête médico-psychologique sur les rapports de la supériorité intellectuelle avec la névropathie. Emile Zola*. Société d'Editions Scientifiques, Paris, 1896. A very curious pre-Freudian analysis based on a thorough examination of Zola by fifteen celebrated medical and psychiatrical specialists (Bertillon, Lombroso, Joffry, Bloch, Huchard, Toulouse, and others).

TRILLING, L., *A Gathering of Fugitives*, Secker & Warburg, London, 1957. Contains an article (12–19) in which this celebrated American critic stresses Zola's fanciful, surrealistic side and suggests affinities with writers and artists like Breughel, Bosch, Ben Jonson, Swift, and Baudelaire.

TURNELL, M., *The Art of French Fiction*, Hamish Hamilton, London, 1959. Includes a chapter on Zola (91–194) treating, among other things, Zola's development of the theme of the fall and redemption and concluding with an analysis of *Le Ventre de Paris*, *L'Assommoir*, *Nana*, *Germinal*, and *La Terre*.

WALKER, P. D., 'The *Ebauche* of *Germinal*', *PMLA*, lxxx (1965), 571–83. An analysis of Zola's original sketch of *Germinal* in his working notes, enumerating the different steps he takes in his methodical development of the dramatic plot, and analysing the different kinds of creative activity involved (scientific, poetic, etc.) in the elaboration of the novel.

—— 'The Octopus and Zola. A New Look', *Symposium*, xxi (1967), 155–65. An attempt to indentify the essential differences between Zola and Norris even in those areas in which they most closely resemble each other.

—— 'Prophetic Myths in Zola', *PMLA*, lxxiv (1959), 444–52. A study of Zola's use of ancient myths of death and resurrection, world destruction and renewal to express an essentially modern vision and portray symbolically the birth of the contemporary world.

—— 'Remarques sur l'image du serpent dans *Germinal*', *Les Cahiers naturalistes*, xxxi (1966), 83–5. An illustration of how Zola's metaphors tend to break free from the objects with which they are originally associated, recurring in association with one or more other objects. The major function of Zola's imagery, it would appear, is not so much to describe elements in the realistic story as to express a poetic vision partly suggested by, and partly imposed on, the realistic subject-matter.

—— 'Zola's art of characterisation in *Germinal*', *L'Esprit Créateur*, iv (1964), 60–70. An analysis and evaluation of Zola's characters considered from two points of view, first as naturalistic portrayals, secondly as abstract creations comparable to many of the abstract human shapes of modern art.

—— 'Zola's use of colour imagery in *Germinal*', *PMLA*, lxxvii (1962), 442–49. A study of the aesthetic functions of colour imagery in *Germinal* showing how, among other things, his use of colour illustrates his definition of his art (in a famous letter to Henry Céard) as a very special kind of lie.

WILSON, A., *Emile Zola. An Introductory study of His Novels*, revised edition, Secker & Warburg, London, 1965. A short, illuminating biographical and critical study undertaken from a predominantly Freudian point of view.

THE PROFILES IN LITERATURE SERIES

GENERAL EDITOR : B. C. SOUTHAM, M.A. B.LITT. (OXON.)
*Formerly Department of English, Westfield College,
University of London*

Volumes in this series include

Emile Zola